Communities That Learn, Lead, and Last

JB JOSSEY-BASS

Communities That Learn, Lead, and Last

BUILDING AND SUSTAINING EDUCATIONAL EXPERTISE

Giselle O. Martin-Kniep

John Wiley & Sons, Inc.

Published by Jossey-Bass
A Wiley Imprint
989 Market Street, San Francisco, CA 94103-1741—www.josseybass.com

Jossey-Bass books and products are available through most bookstores. To contact Jossey-Bass directly call our Customer Care Department within the U.S. at 800-956-7739, outside the U.S. at 317-572-3986, or fax 317-572-4002.

Jossey-Bass also publishes its books in a variety of electronic formats. Some content that appears in print may not be available in electronic books.

Library of Congress Cataloging-in-Publication Data

Martin-Kniep, Giselle O., date
  Communities that learn, lead, and last: building and sustaining educational expertise / Giselle O. Martin-Kniep.—1st ed.
    p. cm.
  Includes bibliographical references and index.
  ISBN 978-0-7879-8513-4 (cloth)
  1. School management teams—United States. 2. Teachers—Professional relationships—United States. 3. Group work in education—United States. I. Title.
  LB2806.3.M27 2008
  371.1—dc22   2007026427

Printed in the United States of America
FIRST EDITION
HB Printing 10 9 8 7 6 5 4 3 2

The Jossey-Bass
Education Series

CONTENTS

FIGURES, TABLES, AND EXHIBITS

FIGURES

TABLES

EXHIBITS

To my mother, for helping me understand what I know

To Richard, for making me question what I know

Why read another book about professional learning communities? There are already many voices speaking to the characteristics and uses of such communities. Some people think that these communities comprise groups of teachers who analyze student work together and use the insights from that analysis to revise lessons. Others propose that a school faculty can be a community, sharing a common vision and purpose. Yet others believe that professional learning communities encompass people from different organizations who work on different activities and projects but share space and time to support each other's work.

I too have a vision for what learning communities are and do, and this book unpacks that vision. What makes it not just another book about learning communities, however, what makes it worth reading in the face of all that has gone before, is that this book has less to do with the who and the what of professional learning communities and far and more to do with the why and the how. It is my hope that this book will contribute to both the big picture of learning communities within the world of educational reform and at the same time provide readers with the means for choosing and achieving the mission of developing such learning communities inside their schools, districts, regions, or other learning organizations.

The work of improving and reforming schools in the United States spans anywhere from fifty to a hundred years, depending on how we define the beginning of that work. Regardless of when we begin, this period is filled with stories of failed attempts. For most of the initiatives and reforms, the story is the same. It takes far less time for a school or a school system to return to where it was prior to the reform it has been subjected to than it does to experience anywhere near the full effect of those reforms. Clearly there are many political, sociological, economic, and historical reasons for this phenomenon. There is one reason that I believe is fundamental to the lack of sustainability of school initiatives and reforms: the story of improving and reforming schools has been primarily about doing and bringing things to them rather than extracting the wisdom they produce.

We learn with others. Our intelligence is derived from our interactions with others. Our ability to make sense of the realities we face, to interact successfully with our environment, to learn from our experiences, is derived from collaborative and collective problem finding and solving. People who work in schools and whose professional lives are about teaching and learning know much about what works, what does not work, and what could work. They have the wisdom of practice. What they do not have are structured and consistent opportunities dedicated to accessing, further developing, and distributing that wisdom.

In schools adults are traditionally isolated from each other in terms of having opportunities for meaningful adult conversations. Yet we crave and need to belong. Our need for affiliation is as great as our need for independence.

Professional learning communities address our need for affiliation and provide practitioners and other individuals who are committed to schools with structures and processes for sharing a social identity, even a cause, and for developing and sharing the wisdom of experience. They offer a missing element in the prevailing approaches to improving schools. By enabling individuals and teams representing all the different roles that focus on the work of schools, with space, time, and processes for identifying, developing, and disseminating their intelligence, they make it possible for schools and districts to address their own problems and needs from within. Professional learning communities are about using the perspectives, successes, missed opportunities, and failed attempts related to making schools places that honor teaching and learning. They are about using the experience and expertise of practitioners as precious resources for individual, social, and organizational learning.

A theory of action frames this book. It holds that professional learning communities that learn, lead, and last can help schools transform themselves into true learning organizations and can produce desired outcomes for the students and adults who inhabit them. They can also promote positive and lasting organizational outcomes within schools and districts. To do so, these communities are supported by tools, processes, and structures that are guided by specific dispositions of practice. The wisdom of practice that educators possess can be tapped in and by these professional learning communities to produce lasting school improvement. Such communities present the opportunity for sustained educational reform because they support reform by educators rather than to educators. This is my vision. Creating, nurturing, assessing, and sustaining professional learning communities in this context are what this book is about.

The title of this book, *Communities That Learn, Lead, and Last,* represents a belief in professional learning communities as evolving and expanding in their self-definition and work. Regardless of how they are formed, how long they exist, or who comprises them, their primary purpose is to improve teaching and learning.

From an evolutionary perspective, these communities comprise individuals who initially are primarily concerned with their own learning. Over time, their work and attention shift toward leading learning and school improvement efforts. At their most mature stage, their learning and leading activities focus on developing the resilience to maintain positive changes and ensuring their sustainability as a learning organization. From this standpoint, leading and lasting result from learning.

As a typology, learning communities can be seen as comprising one or more layers representing the focus of their endeavors, with some communities focused exclusively on learning, others focused on both learning and leading, and yet others incorporating learning and leading in the service of organizational sustainability. Communities that learn can exist independently from those that lead and last, but leading and lasting communities require a simultaneous focus on learning.

The book is organized around eight questions, each one becoming the focus of a chapter plus the conclusion. Chapter One addresses the question: What are professional learning communities, and why should we promote them? This chapter situates professional learning communities in a historical context and offers three different yet intrinsically related arguments for their existence. In this chapter, I have drawn from the wealth of excellent work that preceded my own work around this construct and that has contributed greatly to my understanding of professional learning communities and to the role they play in schools.

Chapter Two focuses on the question: What do we need to understand about professional learning communities? It describes key characteristics of professional learning communities: their focus and membership. It portrays communities as operating within a developmental continuum, much like individuals and organizations. It depicts these development levels as related to specific dispositions of practice evident in communities. These dispositions include a commitment to understanding, intellectual perseverance, courage and initiative, commitment to expertise, commitment to reflection, and collegiality.

Chapter Three deals with the question: How do we develop individual capacity for participating in professional learning communities? It addresses the issue of individual readiness for professional learning communities. Readiness is fluid. It is not something we have or lack but rather something we have some or more of. In our work, readiness and capacity go hand in hand. The readier we are to engage in a certain kind of work, such as using the products of student learning to assess and modify curriculum, the more capacity we have to develop a curriculum that truly addresses students' needs. This chapter is aimed at helping readers recognize stages of readiness for learning communities, use questions to assess it, and explore interventions to promote it.

Chapter Four ponders the question: How do organizations shape and build capacity for professional learning communities? It describes the organizational conditions that support professional learning communities, beginning with an overview of the structures, roles, responsibilities, climate, and other factors that relate to professional learning communities. It elaborates on the ways in which organizations embrace the dispositions of practice discussed in prior chapters and includes questions and interventions to assess and promote greater readiness for professional learning communities.

Chapter Five raises the question: How do we facilitate, manage, evaluate, and sustain professional learning communities? It describes the context and processes that support the work of learning communities, including the role of purpose, membership, facilitators, and participants. It also details the process of setting agendas and the function of dialogue and feedback in enabling community members to produce high-quality work.

Chapter Six ponders the question: What are the outcomes of professional learning communities? It offers a detailed characterization of the tangible and intangible processes and understandings that result from the work of professional learning communities and the products that embody such outcomes. Included in this chapter is a description of the tools and processes that communities can use to guide and support participants' work.

Chapter Seven addresses the question: How do participants in professional learning communities evaluate and monitor their work? It describes the evaluation processes that community members can use to monitor their processes and activities and the development and attainment of the work they produce.

The Conclusion answers one final question: What is the promise of professional learning communities?

Together these chapters represent the composite story of several learning communities I have had the privilege to create and support, and more specifically, the work of the Communities for Learning (formerly known as the Center for the Study of Expertise in Teaching and Learning, or CSETL), where I discovered the power and significance of that construct.

Communities for Learning is a nonprofit organization I founded as a forum for teachers, administrators, staff developers, and university professors to investigate, capture, and disseminate their professional expertise in the service of school improvement. The fifteen individuals who in 1995 were the first cadre of fellows in that center, the individuals who participate in this year's two cadres (one in upstate New York and one on Long Island), and every individual in between have given me compelling evidence that we possess the wisdom to create the schools we would have liked to experience when we were children or wish our children would have.

For ten years, Communities for Learning operated as a program housing several professional learning communities that offered educators of all kinds the opportunity to be thoughtful, to learn from each other, and to create and disseminate experiences and expertise that could make schools better places for all to be. In its current form, Communities for Learning is as much a forum for research and development of professional learning communities as it is a framework for the development of professional learning communities that support adult and student learning. It is a way of operating as much as a process for developing and channeling questions and work. It calls for the practice of specific dispositions that help individuals and organizations think and grow in purposeful and strategic ways.

This book seeks to distill the lessons from observing and studying the work of individual participants in learning communities and of the communities themselves. It also seeks to ground the concept of professional learning communities in something far more robust and important than much of what is currently associated with the words. Finally, it hopes to engage readers in an exploration of the potential role that individuals and groups who are steeped in practice can play in transforming schools into places that honor learning for all.

ACKNOWLEDGMENTS

Writing can be an arduous endeavor at times. Many of my initial attempts at writing this book felt that way because when I sat to draft the first chapters, I was not ready to write. I didn't know then that I needed time to process internally what I wanted to communicate to others and to construct the arguments that still lacked development. I am forever indebted to my dear friend and colleague, Joanne Picone-Zocchia, who developed many of the tools related to professional learning communities, lent me her undivided attention during the writing of this book, and knew when to operate as co-conceptualizer, editor, critic, and, most important, friend.

I am deeply grateful for the friendship and support of Richard Strong and for the inspiration that his wisdom and insight have brought to my life.

Finally, this book could not have been written without many individuals who have co-constructed learning communities with me. They include all the fellows from the Center for the Study of Expertise in Teaching and Learning, now Communities for Learning, as well as the participants in almost ten different three-year design and leadership development programs. I wish I could name them all and hope that this book contributes in some measure to honoring their thinking and their work.

Communities for Learning: Leading Lasting Change is a nonprofit organization established in 1997 and located in Sea Cliff, New York, whose mission is to create professional communities that learn, lead, and last. Originally named the Center for the Study of Expertise in Teaching and Learning (CSETL), this organization has worked to improve the learning of schools as organizations, as well as the adults and students inside them, through the identification, consolidation, and dissemination of educators' expertise and best practice in the context of professional learning communities. Operating itself as a professional learning community functioning at the systemic level, Communities for Learning supports two different fellowship programs where teachers, administrators, professional developers, university faculties, and students reconcile their individual passions and expertise with the vision of the organizations that sponsor them.

Communities for Learning offers a variety of programs and services related to the development and support of professional learning communities. These include readiness assessments; skill-based programs; keynotes and workshops; programs for understanding change; and facilitation of school-based, network, and regional professional learning communities, as well as programs that lead to the certification of a school, district, or region as a Communities for Learning: Leading Lasting Change site.

For further information, contact:

Communities for Learning: Leading Lasting Change
249-02 Jericho Turnpike, Suite 203
Floral Park, NY 11001
516-502-4232 phone
516-502-4233 fax
www.communitiesforlearning.org

THE AUTHOR

Giselle O. Martin-Kniep is a teacher-educator, researcher, program evaluator, and writer. She is the president of Learner-Centered Initiatives, an educational consulting organization specializing in comprehensive regional and school-based curriculum and assessment work. She is also the CEO of the Communities for Learning: Leading Lasting Change, an organization committed to changing schools from within by developing learning communities that lead and last.

Martin-Kniep has a strong background in organizational change and has a master's degree in communication and development, a doctorate in social sciences in education, and a post-doctorate degree in educational evaluation from Stanford University. She has taught at Adelphi University, the University of British Columbia, and the University of Victoria. She has worked with hundreds of schools and districts nationally and internationally in the areas of alternative assessment, standards-based design, school improvement, and action research.

Martin-Kniep has written extensively. Her books include *Why Am I Doing This: Purposeful Teaching with Portfolio Assessment; Capturing the Wisdom of Practice: Portfolios for Teachers and Administrators; Becoming a Better Teacher: Eight Innovations That Work;* and *Developing Learning Communities Through Teacher Expertise.* She is now working on a new book centered on a framework for effective teaching.

Communities That Learn, Lead, and Last

What Are Professional Learning Communities, and Why Should We Promote Them?

There are fifteen people in a room: one-district level and one building-level administrator, six teachers from several different subject areas in grades 6 to 8 and subject areas, two teaching assistants, three students, and two parents. The room is filled with the buzzing sounds of work.

A small group is developing a collaborative presentation for the school board on ways to support the needs of diverse learners in heterogeneous classrooms through developmentally responsive lessons. A district-level administrator, a student, and a teacher are designing a survey for all school members on their perceptions of the new advisory program for the middle school. One teacher is polishing the introduction to an up-coming seventh-grade unit of study on bias. A group of five is listening and providing feedback to the principal as she shares her ideas for a handbook of reading strategies she is proposing to develop and publish. A parent, a teacher, and a student are grappling with reconciling grade-level expectations with state standards so that they can begin to identify language and tools for reporting student progress and achievement with the ultimate goal of revising the report card.

Although the work of individuals and groups may be different, each person in the room is challenged by the idea that he or she has an important role to play in school improvement. Each is focused on articulating or polishing a component of his or her practice for which there is no time set aside in their day-to-day work. While an outsider stopping in for a few minutes might have trouble making sense of what appears to be disjointed work, the group, as a whole, is driven by same purpose: to improve everyone's learning in schools. Tomorrow they will all go back to their routines, carrying with them the impact of today's learning.

I cannot think of any other profession that is subject to the kinds of demands that teaching faces. These demands are no less than revolutionary, and they explain, to a great extent, the enormous challenge of improving schools. They also provide the context and rationale for professional learning communities.

First, our understanding of how students learn best and of what they need to learn to function in life and in society imposes the demand that teachers become adept at diagnosing and addressing individual student needs and that they adopt a pedagogy that enables them to do so. For example, current scientific understandings about brain functions and how these affect the kinds of reading problems students face demand that teachers strategically select and try different approaches for helping individual students interact with the written word.

Second, teacher preparation programs face the increasing challenge of producing graduates who are able to cope with conditions, structures, and contradictions in schools that have not been reflected in the content or pedagogy of the preservice or even in-service curriculum they offer; the result is that graduates are at a deficit before they even get started teaching. Today's novice teachers are not generally prepared to respond to increasing school demands, such as addressing state and national standards in their lessons and assessments or teaching in ways that support the learning needs of all the different students they teach. Nor are they prepared to adapt to changes resulting from the adoption of new programs and curricula, or of programs that require instructional approaches such as differentiated instruction, while at the same time implementing a fairly structured basal reading series.

Third, although significant attention has been paid to articulating and operationalizing content and state standards, there has not been a parallel effort to help schools or teachers determine how to use them to help make decisions about what to teach or assess.

Fourth, although schools often respond to the need to adopt and use textbooks and educational resources that are aligned with standards, they provide little support to teachers in tailoring these resources to their own and their students' needs.

Finally, schools are structured in a way that minimizes collaboration, reflection, and innovation, the very elements that support meeting these demands.

When new demands are placed on other professions, they are often accompanied by a large investment of human and technical support to facilitate the transition from current to desired knowledge and practice. Most schools, however, lack the resources for professional development that are required for teachers to be effective facilitators and assessors of learning. In light of these deficits, it is truly remarkable that many schools have teachers who are well versed in the facilitation of student learning, knowledgeable and skilled in teaching a standards-based curriculum, and able to work effectively within and outside the classroom.

In the United States, we seem to lack the political will to accept that if we want schools to do what they need to do, we need to strengthen their core. We have to stop measuring their deficits through outside tests and means, and build their capacity and resilience to operate as learning organizations, where learning by students and adults is their most prized commodity. This is where professional learning communities offer a viable and promising approach to improving student learning in schools.

Schools will improve if and when many more teachers can help students learn. Teachers can help students learn best when they have the knowledge, skills, and dispositions to make that happen; when they see themselves as learners; when they are supported by structures that value their learning as well as student learning; and when they can work in forums in which students and others can inform their decision making and other practices. Education—and its practitioners—need the context, content, time, and processes to support learning; develop knowledge, skills, and dispositions that promote inquiry around practice; and evidence a value for the learning and contributions of its members, adult and child alike. Such is the promise of professional learning communities.

WHAT DO WE MEAN BY PROFESSIONAL LEARNING COMMUNITIES?

The term *professional learning community* is as popular now as the terms *restructuring, cooperative learning, alternative assessment,* and *outcomes-based education* have been in years past. Like these and other terms, it runs the risk of becoming one more fad in the history of educational reform. Those of us who work in or for schools have seen many of these fads come and go without leaving much of a legacy. My intent is to demonstrate in this book that when professional learning communities are treated seriously and supported adequately, they have the potential to greatly improve the lives of students and educators.

As is the case in other disciplines, the field of education borrows, steals, adopts, and even invents its own terminology, often using old words in new ways or to convey new meaning. We are probably not as careful as we should be in defining the terms we use or even in applying such terms in similar ways across contexts. The term *learning community* is one such term. It has been used over two decades and has recently been popularized and used in schools and other contexts to describe several different arrangements and structures (Brandt, 2004; DuFour, DuFour, Eaker, and Many, 2006; Hargreaves, 2003; Hord, 2004; Lieberman and Miller, 2004; Little, 2003; McLaughlin and Talbert, 2001; Ross and Gray, 2006; Senge, 1990; Shulman, 2004; Wenger, 1998). Interestingly enough, earlier uses of the term are broader and deeper than some of the current characterizations. Some emphasize the players, whereas others emphasize the work that the community produces or what the community represents. Table 1.1 shows how different authors have defined professional learning communities in terms of their participants and purposes over time.

Each definition of *professional learning community* has, over the years, contributed to our overall understanding, yet these communities remain complex and fairly elusive as a concept and a practice—complex because they supersede formal organizational structures, which can evolve over time in their focus and work, and elusive because the very name is composed of three terms (*professional, learning,* and *community*), each with many different connotations, any combination of which changes the essence of the whole.

In the context of this book, professional learning communities are forums in which participants embrace the privilege and responsibility of learning individually and collectively. Their purpose is to improve their own thinking and practice

Table 1.1
Selected Characterizations of Learning Communities

Author	Who Is Included?	What Is Their Purpose?
Shulman (2004)	Collegium or setting where individuals who are peers come together with a shared mission	Overcome the limitations of individual experience and understanding in the absence of multiple perspectives, by having practitioners access, share, and negotiate each other's wisdom of practice
Senge (1990)	People in the organization who see the need for change in the business community	Effect positive change
Sergiovanni (1994)	Collections of individuals who share ideas and beliefs	Do things differently, develop new kinds of relationships, create new ties, make new commitments
Brandt (2004)	Individuals who are responsible for their actions, while at the same time embracing the common good	Harness individual talent and commitment to a group effort that pushes for high-quality learning for all students
Wenger (1998)	Members who join in common activities and learn together through the relationships with other people	Affect performance, handle unstructured problems, and share knowledge outside traditional structural boundaries
Capers (2004)	Teachers who share, identify, articulate, and communicate—to themselves, each other, and the public at large—the practices and procedures that facilitate learning and characterize excellent instruction	Provide the ground on which standards are observed and developed, the means by which they are conveyed, and the structures through which they are enforced on a school-by-school basis
Munro (2005)	Individuals who have a shared commitment to agreed-on community goals and shared learning, including ongoing collaboration and communication among members	Enhanced teacher practice and improved student learning
DuFour, Eaker, and DuFour (2005)	Groups of educators committed to working collaboratively in ongoing processes of collective inquiry and action research	Achieve better results for students by pondering the questions: What is it we want students to learn? How will we know if they have learned it? What will we do if they do not learn it?

in the service of supporting adult and student learning in the organizations they work for. They include one or more cross-sections of educators and administrators in a school, a school district, or an educational organization who seek to address significant problems related to teaching, learning, and the other work of schools. Participants include teachers, administrators, students, professional developers, and other educators or school specialists. The cross-role structure of the group is critical for two reasons. First, it enables the community to explore and understand multiple perspectives related to teaching, learning, and the other work of schools. Second, it depoliticizes the community by allowing its members to transcend individual or role-specific concerns in order to explore critical issues of practice. Although the individual questions and pursuits of participants may be different, together they share a purpose, a vision, and one or more goals that relate to making the school a learning organization, where inquiry and the pursuit of new understandings are common to all. Their common purpose, vision, and goals are fostered by the belief that they are knowledge producers, or generators, who investigate, document, and publish some aspect of their expertise and experience.

Collegial inquiry and reflective practice are the language and the sustenance of professional learning communities. They provide participants with the opportunity to articulate and analyze their thinking and their practices, reconcile individual questions and issues with organizational needs, compare contexts and situations and find meaningful patterns, and search for the big picture without losing sight of particulars.

What would such communities look like? Let's return to the scenario at the beginning of the chapter.

The group of fifteen comes together in five different occasions during the year for one to two days each time. They bring with them their roles and experiences but leave behind the politics of their own contexts. The community provides them with ample space for articulating their perspective but little room for including the minutia of their day-to-day work-related existence. In their shared collective space, they ask questions about their work and the organizations they represent, and they study alone and together, sometimes relying on books and research and at other times analyzing each other's practices. They spend time discussing specific texts and pondering the implications for their roles and responsibilities. They write and revise, only to write and revise again. They constantly negotiate the goals and needs that drive their work in the community, aware of the importance of their caring deeply about such work, but mindful that it must link to or address an organization need or goal. They use the community as a forum to think, negotiate, and create. They use it as a place where they can deepen their understandings about teaching and learning, improve their professional craft, and revise their practices. Figure 1.1 provides an example from Wanda Alsheimer, a second grade teacher in upstate New York who analyzed changes in her practices over a three-year period stemming from her participation in a learning community. Professional learning communities recognize the time and space they occupy in the community as a gift.

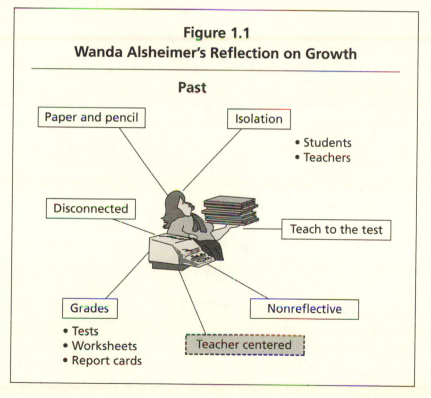

Figure 1.1
Wanda Alsheimer's Reflection on Growth

Past

Paper and pencil

Isolation

• Students
• Teachers

Disconnected

Teach to the test

Grades

• Tests
• Worksheets
• Report cards

Nonreflective

Teacher centered

(Continued)

Figure 1.1 (*Continued*)

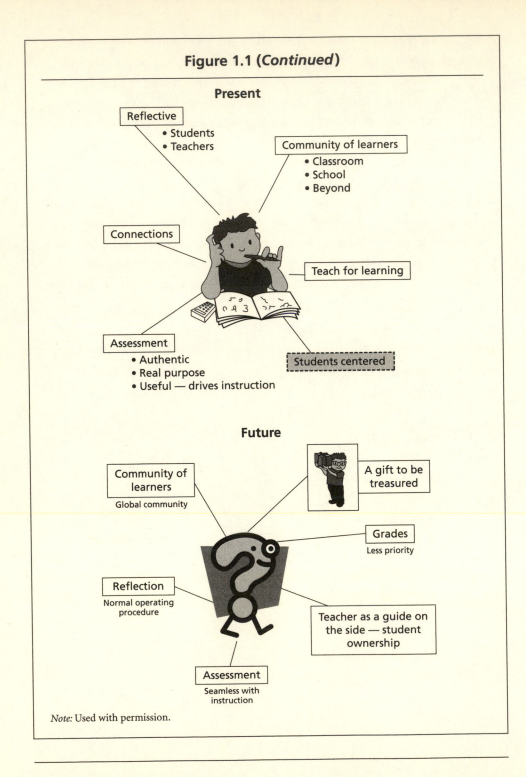

Present

Reflective
- Students
- Teachers

Community of learners
- Classroom
- School
- Beyond

Connections

Teach for learning

Assessment
- Authentic
- Real purpose
- Useful — drives instruction

Students centered

Future

Community of learners

Global community

A gift to be treasured

Grades

Less priority

Reflection

Normal operating procedure

Teacher as a guide on the side — student ownership

Assessment

Seamless with instruction

Note: Used with permission.

WHY SHOULD WE PROMOTE PROFESSIONAL LEARNING COMMUNITIES?

The primary underlying tenet of professional learning communities is that expertise in teaching and learning abounds, but the current structure of the educational profession has precluded our capacity to access, use, and disseminate it as well as we could.

There are at least three related sets of arguments for the creation of professional learning communities. One relates to their effect on students, a second one to the outcomes they produce in teachers, and the third to their function in schools. Despite the fact that some of these arguments have been enunciated far more than others, all three are critical if professional learning communities are to have a sustainable and significant impact on the lives of teachers and students. Most important is that these three arguments are interdependent and need to be considered in a systemic and strategic fashion if professional learning communities are to be more than another fad or event in the life of schools.

Learning Communities Benefit Students

The most frequently used argument for learning communities is that these communities can lead to improved student learning by enhancing teachers' knowledge and skills. In other words, learning communities increase teachers' learning, and that in turn translates into increased student learning.

A growing body of research establishes a direct link between teacher quality and student learning (Byme, 1983; Darling-Hammond, 2003). According to Darling-Hammond (2003) "teacher expertise is one of the most important school factors influencing student achievement, far outweighing the lesser but generally positive influences of small schools and small class sizes" (p. 77). "A study comparing high-achieving and low-achieving schools found that 90 percent of the variation in student achievement in mathematics and reading could be traced to teacher qualifications. Other research found that recruiting and developing more highly qualified teachers is the most cost-effective means of improving student achievement" (National Commission on Teaching and America's Future, 1996, p. 161). Another study showed that "in just one academic year, the top third of teachers produced as much as six times the learning growth of the bottom third" (Sparks, 2005, p. 47). Research by Bandura (1993) indicates that student achievement is significantly and positively related to collective teacher efficacy and that collective teacher efficacy has a greater effect on student achievement than does student socioeconomic level. Another study found that "collective teacher efficacy was positively associated with differences between schools in student-achievement in both reading and mathematics" (Goddard, Hoy, and Hoy, 2000, p. 479). Research by Silins and Mulford (2004) suggests that teachers who work in schools that operate as learning organizations produce higher levels of student participation and engagement in learning.

Increasing teacher expertise clearly lies at the heart of improving student outcomes. Improving expertise is no small matter since teaching requires far more than acquiring technical skills; among the necessary categories of knowledge and skills are these:

- Content knowledge (what to teach)

- Pedagogical knowledge (how to teach)

- Pedagogical content-specific knowledge (how to teach subject-specific material)

- Curriculum design knowledge (how to craft and implement learning experiences)

- Assessment design knowledge (what to assess) and assessment skills (how and when to assess)

- Classroom management skills

- Intrapersonal or self-understanding (reflectivity)

- Interpersonal skills (how to relate to students, peers, parents, and others)

- Practical knowledge (about parents, schools, colleagues, and school, for example)

Professional learning communities can be a means to increasing teachers' expertise, which is the most direct path to improved learning for students.

Teaching so that all students learn to achieve at high levels requires that teachers understand how students learn; that they plan and design lessons that enable all students to attain desired outcomes and that such lessons account for differences in their background, skills, or dispositions; that they diagnose students' learning needs and use that information as the basis for curriculum planning; and that they use varied assessment practices that enable students to demonstrate their learning of content, skills, and habits of mind.

Such teaching and learning cannot be prepackaged, neatly structured into pacing guides, or reduced to teacher-proofed curriculum consisting in scripted lessons that bypass teachers' knowledge and expertise. Now more than ever before, teaching requires collegial structures that enable teachers to articulate, refine, negotiate, question, and share their expertise and practice so that they can benefit students. Professional learning communities can become structures that lead to the improvement of student learning.

When learning communities include students as members, students can benefit by joining adult conversations in which their insights related to teaching and learning are respected and valued. These communities can also help students learn about perspectives related to teaching and learning that they do not hear in the classroom, and participate in democratic forms of discourse.

Learning Communities Benefit Teachers

The second and related argument for the creation of learning communities relates to their value for teachers' learning and work. Teaching is a highly complex professional endeavor involving science, craft, and art, often simultaneously. Its complexity lies in the facts that no single practice works for every student; that it is difficult at best to tailor specific instructional and assessment approaches to the needs and interests of different students; and that despite decades of standards, there is a wide range of understandings about desirable learning outcomes.

Lee Shulman's instrumental work around teacher expertise (2004) provides compelling arguments for the role that professional learning communities can have in terms of helping teachers transcend the limitations of their individual practice. Individual teachers have difficulties articulating, understanding, and internalizing specific practices and events without either the assistance of colleagues who can help them observe or monitor their own teaching behavior or a system for record keeping or reporting. Teaching occurs at too fast a pace, with little room for recovery, processing, or revisiting future courses of action based on past and current events. For the most part, teachers' work revolves around dealing with specific lessons, issues, and students.

These working conditions create the need for forums where teachers can learn from each other, share their experiences with other teachers related to individual incidents and students in order to derive sound generalizations about effective practice, and improve their thinking and work. Because learning is primarily a social process and human beings construct their understanding about what they learn through social discourse (Vygotsky, 1962), professional learning communities can provide the means to support the development of a shared and collective expertise about teaching and learning. They can offer teachers opportunities to negotiate the meaning of what they know in the same kinds of social environments that students require. When these communities include students, teachers can deepen their understanding of their own practices by testing their assumptions with students and learning from students' own insights, questions, and assumptions about teaching and learning.

To the extent that we will always be limited by our own context and experience, we need to figure out ways of sharing what we know and understand so that collectively we can become wiser. Shulman and Carey's work on bounded and collective rationality (2004) suggests that only through shared learning can teachers come to understand things in depth and transcend the limitations of their unique and individual perspective. Collectively teachers can find answers to questions and insights into issues that as individuals they find difficult to understand.

Despite the fact that teacher induction programs of one sort or another exist in many schools, all teachers, and especially new teachers, lack organizational support structures that enable them to learn what they need to know about teaching and learning in order to be effective practitioners. More often than not, learning the craft of teaching is a solitary pursuit that is enhanced when a teacher has the good fortune to be close enough to one or more role models. The American Federation of Teachers (Robinson, 1985), the Task Force on Teaching as a Profession (Carnegie Forum on Education and the Economy, 1986), and Capers (2004) have reached some consensus regarding the conditions that characterize teaching as a profession. "Based on this general consensus," writes Capers (2004), "a profession can be defined by four broad categories: critical self-consciousness, practical expertise, trustful client relationships, and collegial regulation— including shared personal practice" (p. 155). Ironically most schools today are structured and function in ways that minimize, if not preclude, the conditions needed for strengthening the professionalization of teaching.

Professional learning communities support teaching as a profession by enabling teachers to explicitly describe and discuss their practices and the decisions that inform them. The critical self-consciousness that emerges from this shared discourse can help them grapple with some of the complexities of the profession. One such complexity lies in the reconciliation of teachers' role as coaches with their role as evaluators. Practical expertise can be fostered through the shared analysis of teachers' approaches to curriculum design, instruction, and assessment. Trust-based collegial relationships can be supported when teachers engage in a continuous dialogue with other practitioners and educators who hold different roles and perspectives but share a common purpose.

Recent statistics on the increasing deskilling of teachers in U.S. schools underscore the need for professional learning communities and remind us of the critical need for preservice and in-service mechanisms to support teachers in developing their professional identities. In addition, "almost one third of teachers exit the field within their first three years; one half leave by the end of the fifth. The result of this exodus is that for the first time in American history, the number of teachers leaving the profession is exceeding the number who is entering the profession" (Lieberman and Miller, 2004, p. 5). Although there are many explanations for this attrition, several of them relate to the ways in which teachers are socialized and supported in their formative years. They also underscore the importance of creating supportive structures within schools, such as professional learning communities in which newer teachers can be mentored and supported during their first three years as teachers and in which more veteran teachers can have a forum for sharing the wisdom of their practice. Such structures may include pairing new with experienced teachers so that the experienced teacher can help the new teacher develop a portfolio of her work and learning over the first two years in the school, peer coaching opportunities, and cross-visitations of classrooms followed by opportunities to debrief and learn from classroom observations.

Now more than ever before, we need to find ways of harnessing the expertise of teachers and using it to inform school improvement and the sound implementation of educational programs and processes aimed at supporting student learning.

Learning Communities Benefit Schools

The third argument for the creation of learning communities relates to their potential role in supporting schools. From an organizational standpoint, several decades of failed attempts at school reform indicate that we need to reconceptualize what we mean by an "effective school system" and rethink the roles within it. School improvement efforts tend to be driven and promoted by entities or organizations outside schools and continue to rely on professional development models that rarely leave any lasting mark.

Notwithstanding the fact that outside consultants and facilitators can and do initiate positive school-based changes and learning processes, outsiders are not likely to sustain progress in the absence of an internal structure that incorporates and internalizes the changes made. Changes in administration, policies, and programs further hinder the sustainability of outside-driven innovations. Professional learning communities have the potential for increasing the resilience of individuals to adapt to leadership and other changes in schools and develop an internal structure for sustaining change and learning in schools.

There is increasing evidence that professional learning communities and collaborative structures have a strong impact on positive outcomes for schools (e. g., Fieman-Nemser and Floden, 1986; Hargreaves and Macmillan, 1991; Little, 1989).

According to Darling-Hammond (2003), what we need is a complete transformation of teaching and the organizational structure of schools into learning organizations where capacity can be cultivated from within and professional talent can be sought, recognized, articulated, and disseminated. The transformation that schools demand requires that we rethink the way we attract, prepare, support, and develop administrators so that they can become the kinds of leaders who understand and know how to leverage teachers' expertise. Ross and Gray's research (2006) supports Darling-Hammond, with evidence that transformational leadership has an impact on the collective teacher efficacy of the school.

School improvement is intrinsically tied to leadership. Professional learning communities can foster the creation and implementation of leadership structures, procedures, and programs that enable the school, as an organization, to develop and fulfill its mission through inquiry and shared leadership rather than through compliance or managed work.

While it is clear that the role of principals is instrumental in the effective management of schools, the complex nature of schools and the increased demands placed on them promote the consideration of distributed leadership structures, as defined by Spillane (2006), where the principal and other adults within the building address issues related to policies, programs, practices, and processes.

True learning communities position the adults (teachers, principals, and other professional staff), and the children within them, as active learners who are constantly in the process of meaning making and knowledge negotiation. Learning becomes a shared endeavor, prized above anything else. It lies at the core of the work of the community.

Schools are rapidly losing the wisdom of practice of teachers and administrators who are retiring and are depleting them of the one asset that can make the most difference in the lives of students: good practitioners who know and understand teaching, learning, and schools. School-based professional learning communities structured in ways that honor everyone's expertise can address this problem by providing teachers, administrators, other school specialists, and other adults who share a commitment to improving schools with mechanisms for knowledge creation and dissemination, enabling them to unpack and refine the wisdom of school practice. As Shulman (1987) stated so eloquently, they allow individuals who work in or for schools "to see the world as they see it, then to understand the manner in which experts construct their problem spaces, their definitions of situations, thus permitting them to act as they do" (p. 257).

The usual organization of schools today, characterized by teacher and principal isolation, minimizes knowledge creation and prevents schools from capitalizing on its primary asset: teachers' expertise. By encouraging practitioners to revisit and articulate the meaning and consequences of their experiences, professional learning communities become the means through which teachers and administrators can maximize what they have learned as individuals, while identifying, consolidating, and sharing best practices. In so doing, they can increase what Goddard, Hoy, and Hoy (2000) have identified in a school reform study as "collective efficacy"—a sense that educators who work together can transform schools.

Professional organizations such as the National Board for Professional Teacher Standards (2001) and studies disseminated by the National Commission for Teaching and America's Future have recognized the relationship between increasing teachers' capacity and the creation of learning communities. They support professional learning communities, arguing for the need to "reinvent . . . professional development," "encourage and support teacher knowledge and skills," and "create schools that are organized for student and teacher success" (Capers, 2004, p. 160). Organizing schools for teacher and student success requires that we tinker with the current roles ascribed to teachers and administrators and rethink leadership structures in ways that maximize collective problem solving and shared accountability for the effective functioning of schools.

WHY WE NEED ALL THREE ARGUMENTS

Each of the arguments for the creation of learning communities is critical. Although the potential for learning communities to benefit students is of great merit, isolating it from the role that learning communities can play in supporting teachers as professionals and schools as organizational entities is at best naive. In fact, much of the literature about learning communities suffers from myopia in that the arguments for their creation often have a single focus and are narrow in scope. In our efforts to find the culprit and take charge, we create learning communities to solve a specific problem, such as using student data to drive instructional decisions related to increasing their success on standardized tests, or develop a formal mechanism for the induction of new teachers. Such interventions, however worthy, assume either that professional learning communities are temporary structures serving single purposes or that they are a permanent fixture to organize the work of teachers.

True professional learning communities assume that their members have valuable experience and expertise to contribute. They value the wisdom of practice that Lee Shulman has often described in his work. They operate from a strength-based perspective and assume that each individual is an asset to the community. They understand that the community is as rich as its members and that the most important activity they can engage in is to learn with and from each other.

Professional learning communities can address and solve specific problems related to programs, policies, and practices. But they can also do and be much more. They offer the promise of new organizational cultures and contexts for the schools we have. They provide mechanisms for capturing practitioners' current expertise and for the creation of new knowledge and understandings. They help us develop new and shared forms of leadership that can result in a collective sense of purpose and accountability for school outcomes. "Professional learning communities writ large means *changing cultures to create new contexts.* . . . The key to this involves conceptualizing sustainability and using leadership to change context or the environment by (1) increasing leaders' participation in wider contexts and

(2) helping to develop leadership in others so they can do the same" (Fullan, 2005, p. 218). Professional learning communities entail new structures for the distribution and dissemination of individual and organizational intelligence.

Professional learning communities are necessary if we want schools to improve and become settings in which teaching and learning are considered prized commodities. They promote environments in which students' minds and bodies are considered in the planning, design, implementation, and evaluation of curriculum; in which teachers are able to negotiate and prioritize the vastness of what they have to teach so as to create lessons and assessments that hang together well—lessons whose purposes are transparent and whose outcomes are the learning that was intended and assessments that capture the wide range of outcomes that rich curricula possess. They can help teachers, administrators, researchers, students, university faculty, board members, and others become part of a community of learners and thinkers who share a purpose and mission and whose work together can make their individual work and perspective far better and more important than it would be if they were not a part of such community.

The Purposes and Dispositions of Professional Learning Communities

Not all learning communities are the same. Consider the following scenario.

It is 3:15 P.M., and a small group of administrators, six classroom teachers, and two special education teachers convene in the staff cafeteria to discuss progress around a comprehensive literacy initiative that includes curriculum, instruction, and assessment design, as well as the analysis of teacher and student work. Sandra Dyers, the principal, calls the meeting to order and asks Joan Saxby, the English department chair, to give a summary of the group's past month's literacy-related activities. Joan begins by describing work that selected teachers from grades 6 to 8 have done around the implementation of writing strategies. She asks Ron Fields, a sixth grade teacher, to describe his own work with students. Ron shares two strategies he has been using to help students elaborate on their writing and how these strategies are affecting the pacing of his lessons. He then describes the specific assignments he used, the way in which he used each strategy, and how he assessed its effectiveness for different types of learners. After all six teachers in the group relate their work around literacy strategies, the group divides into triads to collectively examine and analyze student work samples stemming from teachers' use of these strategies. Some of the questions that the triads ponder as they analyze the student work include: How did the strategies affect different learners and the work they produced? What was the impact of the strategy on the quality of the work? and Are there any unintended consequences of using the strategies in the way they were used?

At 4:45 P.M., Dyers asks the group what they think they need to accomplish by the next monthly meeting. The group brainstorms various ideas, which she writes down. She then tells the group that she will think about these ideas and get back to them in a couple of days with her decision about next steps.

This scenario depicts a professional learning community at work. During the meeting, the principal and teachers engaged in a collective exploration of literacy practices that drew out the explicit identification of individual assumptions about teaching and learning. They had a collective experience that included finding and addressing problems related to the use of specific literacy strategies and fostered their reflection on the merits, shortcomings, and implications of those strategies.

Let's examine another scenario:

A school district has recently completed a process that led to the identification of its vision and mission. As an outgrowth of that work, the superintendent has invited interested individuals, including teachers, administrators, board members, and parents, to explore differentiated instruction and concept-based learning. A group of twenty-four individuals—thirteen teachers, two parents, one board member, and eight administrators, including the assistant superintendent—meet for an afternoon once a month during the school year. Sometimes they read articles and books and discuss them as a large group. At other times, they work individually or in small groups articulating or designing strategies to address the needs of specific students; reviewing existing curriculum and instructional materials in terms of their relevance to particular groups of students; exploring concept-based units for specific subjects and grades; and analyzing multiple sources of data related to teachers' grading practices and their impact on students.

At the end of the year, the superintendent meets with the group to learn their findings and recommendations. The group shares as many findings and proposals as they raise new questions and concerns related to student needs. They decide to make their gatherings an ongoing structure for practitioners, parents, and community members to explore and address issues and problems related to teaching and learning.

Purpose is a key variable differentiating learning communities. Some communities are primarily focused on supporting the learning of their participants by developing their individual understandings, skills, strategies, and processes. These are *communities that learn.* The communities in the two scenarios are examples. Their explicit emphasis is to provide opportunities for everyone to learn and to build on their experience by contributing to their professional expertise. Although one is a school-based community and the other is district based, the members of both communities are clearly committed to deepening their understanding of teaching and learning and to exploring and addressing specific issues and problems important to teaching and learning. These communities seek, first and foremost, to learn. Although others outside the professional learning community may be influenced by their learning, affecting others is not the primary intent of a community that learns.

In these communities, learning is clearly tied to individual backgrounds, interests, and needs. It is also shared and connected to the schools' needs to support students' learning resulting from the implementation of specific writing strategies.

To facilitate everyone's learning, participants in these communities:

- Learn from their experiences and deepen their understandings
- Surface and test assumptions that arise from their learning
- Develop the dispositions (abiding tendencies that reflect the values, commitments, practices, and professional ethics that influence behaviors and actions) and values that promote professional learning communities
- Ponder questions of mission and purpose as they relate to themselves and their work

- Identify and consider short- and long-term consequences of their actions
- Recognize the unintended consequences of their actions
- Explore complex cause-and-effect relationships in their actions and in the actions of those they affect
- Find and understand optimum entry points for their actions
- Manage internal and external dissonance that stems from their learning experiences

Other learning communities are concerned with developing the leadership capacity of their members. These communities steer the learning of individual participants and the community as a whole toward developing understandings, skills, strategies, and processes to support or facilitate the learning of other adults inside the school, district, or other educational organization. In these communities, participants see their learning as instrumental to the common need of leading—hence, their name: *communities that lead.* Such a community is depicted in the following scenario.

A large school district has made a strong commitment to improving teacher and student learning. As part of a five-year district redesign plan, a cabinet composed of the superintendent and his central office staff and its board identify key long-term initiatives, one of which is curriculum coherence. The cabinet solicits an open invitation to the entire district for its input. It forms a design team comprising interested district and building administrators, content specialists, and teachers who work side by side with an educational consultant to develop self-contained but interrelated professional development modules on different aspects of teaching and learning. Three to five modules are designed and implemented each year to enhance teachers' practices related to curriculum, instruction, and assessment.

In its efforts to reach every teacher in the system and ensure the quality of both delivery and implementation of these modules, the district creates multiple groups or cadres of facilitators. Each school is asked to invite a team of interested teachers, coaches, and administrators to participate in a multiday exploration of the content of each module and the processes that support teachers' learning and implementation. These cadres have several opportunities to learn and practice the content and processes of the modules and are supported with guided and independent opportunities to practice facilitating them, getting feedback on the quality of their facilitation. The cadres are ultimately able to use these modules to effect changes in teachers' practices and in student learning. As the cadres continue to meet in their own community, their learning deepens as a result of their shared discourse around the implementation of the modules.

This example illustrates a professional learning community that learns and leads: the members learn much in the context of their participation, and then they direct their learning at influencing the work of other outside groups of teachers, that is, their community.

In addition to promoting the development of specific dispositions and values, these communities provide participants with learning opportunities that focus on leadership development—for example:

- Learning to lead
- Surfacing and testing assumptions that arise from their learning about leading
- Pondering questions of mission and purpose as they relate to leading
- Recognizing the short-term, long-term, and unintended consequences of their actions related to leading
- Exploring complex cause-and-effect relationships that stem from their leadership work
- Looking for and identifying interdependencies in their work and in the work of those they lead
- Managing the dissonance that stems from learning to lead
- Finding and understanding optimum entry points for their work related to leading

Finally, there are other learning communities that understand and value their learning as instrumental to leading others, but whose overall focus is to promote resilience of their school or system to sustain positive changes and operate as a learning organization. These communities delve deeply into the study of change processes and underscore the importance of helping their organization and its members engage in reasoned adaptation processes toward desired outcomes. In these communities, which I refer to as *communities that last,* questions of mission and purpose coexist with changes in leadership, and significant emphasis is placed on developing mechanisms, structures, and practices that promote learning for all adults and students.

Some of the learning opportunities that communities that last provide their members share similarities with those provided by communities that learn and lead, and others are different. The following are unique to communities that last:

- Pondering questions of mission and purpose as they relate to their organization

- Seeking an understanding of their organization's big picture

- Recognizing unintended consequences where they emerge in their own, others', and the organization's actions

- Looking for and identifying interdependencies in their own work and in the work of the organization

- Exploring complex cause-and-effect relationships in the organization's processes, practices, policies, programs, and structures

- Finding and understanding optimum entry points for their actions related to the organization

- Supporting the work of surviving changes in leadership, membership, governing policies, and other areas

Communities that last and communities that lead are nested inside communities that learn, so all three communities have learning at their core. But not all communities that learn either evolve into or are ever designed to become communities that lead, and not all communities that lead mature into or are designed to function as communities that last (see Figure 2.1).

Professional learning communities are results focused and goal oriented and mission and passion driven. Given their different purposes, they vary in the learning opportunities and experiences they provide to members. They also vary in

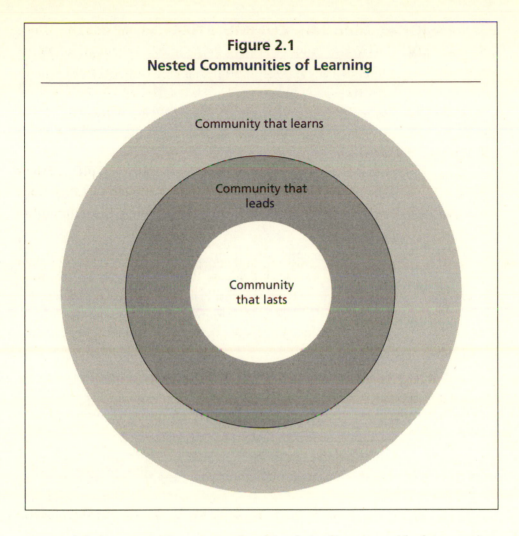

**Figure 2.1
Nested Communities of Learning**

Community that learns

Community that
leads

Community
that lasts

terms of their composition or membership, their alignment with the organizations that support them, their stability, and their endurance.

In some of these learning communities, individuals share roles and responsibilities, whereas others are designed to maximize heterogeneity in terms of roles, experience, and position inside their system. Some communities include only individuals who work in the same school or system, whereas others comprise people who work in different schools or even different organizations. Some include students as members, and some include students only in terms of the focus of the community's work.

PROFESSIONAL LEARNING COMMUNITIES EVOLVE OVER TIME

Regardless of their overall focus and membership, all professional learning communities evolve and mature as social entities. They have developmental levels that can be described in terms of a continuum of behaviors, beliefs, and practices that depict their readiness or capacity to operate, support, and function as learning communities. The continuum has four levels—beginning, developing, established, and systemic—that apply equally to communities that learn, lead, and last. Similarly, the individuals who comprise them and the organizations that support them also operate at different levels of readiness in their participation and support of learning communities.

As with any other developmental continuum, each level contains a range of behaviors and manifestations so that individuals, organizations, and communities can be in different phases of development. It is possible that a community operates at a given level but that the organization in which it is housed is at a different level or that the individuals who comprise it are distributed far more broadly along the continuum.

At a beginning level, community members have a sense of themselves with regard to the school or system in which they live and recognize that they have some voice in that system, but they do not play an active role or assume responsibility for actions other than their own. They are aware of the contributions others can make to their thinking or work, but seek to work and think on their own or with colleagues with whom they share affinities, roles, and responsibilities. Members of these communities have a sense of purpose that is defined in terms of the people they have a direct impact on, for example, a teacher's students or a principal's staff. Communities operating at this level tend to focus on tasks that are role specific or have a clear beginning and end.

At a developing level, community members have internalized the importance of cultivating their expertise and learning with others. They are aware of the school's needs and view their self-improvement as a means to address them. Participants in these communities are willing to assume some responsibility for the work of the community and are open to considering changes in their own practices or in their system, although they tend to support these only when they build on current practice and reality and are incremental. Sandra Dyers's community is operating at this level.

Learning communities that are at a developing level seek and value the participation of their members in the pursuit of goals that address the community's and organizational needs. These communities tend to include people who have diverse roles and perspectives, often organized into committees or task groups that tackle specific problems or innovations. The emphasis of these communities is on learning from each other as they work together on common tasks.

When members of the learning community operate at the established level, they connect their individual work and behavior to their organization. They understand and appreciate the importance of working with others to improve teaching and learning. They participate in opportunities to learn and work with others within and outside their own roles and experiences. They value being a part of their organization and playing an active role in improving it. Communities that function at this level link the work of the community to the organizational vision. They explore organizational problems and needs by accessing people who have different perspectives and positions in their system and seek to learn with them from the past to understand the present.

Let's return to the scenario of the district-wide learning community that invested in the creation of leadership cadres that learned about and delivered curriculum modules. If that community evolved to an established level, its members would be deepening and refining their facilitation skills and their understanding of curriculum by developing, implementing, and assessing new learning experiences for adults in consultation with teachers and administrators from their respective schools to ensure that their leadership work addressed the specific needs of their schools.

The systemic level is characterized by grounded and reflective practice for both individuals and learning communities. Members of these communities see their community as a significant player in school improvement with a deep commitment to making their organization a learning enterprise for all. Self-improvement and organizational improvement are deeply connected. Communities at this level nurture a shared commitment to improving teaching and learning for all. They invest heavily in understanding the school as a complex system and in carefully devising processes for understanding and addressing its goals and needs, including maximizing the strengths and experiences of all members of the community. Participants in these communities use needs assessments, scenario planning, systems thinking, and other tools to understand and assess their current realities, sustain good work, and create the conditions for a desired future.

Like other social entities, professional learning communities may evolve from one stage of development to another over time. They may also be terminated or cease to function, especially at the early stages of their development. Although communities that operate at a systemic level are far more resilient than communities operating at other levels, they too can lose resilience, regress to a previous level, and finally dissolve. This could happen with a major shift in policy at the board level, for example, or with the concurrent onset of teacher retirements and the replacement of an administrative cabinet.

Finally, not all individuals and organizations are poised to support professional learning communities, although they may want to. For example, individuals who would otherwise be part of a community may operate in isolation of each other, either because they are actually separate from each other or because they seek such isolation. This is the case when teachers are reluctant to open their classrooms to other adults or when principals have a closed-door policy, using compliance as a driver to steer teachers away from them. Organizations that are not yet ready to support learning communities prefer hierarchical power structures and tend to value compliance and efficiency. Many of these organizations often act as though they were in a state of perpetual crisis.

Even in situations where readiness may not be apparent but there is an interest in professional learning communities, it is possible to design and implement specific interventions to help develop the necessary conditions for professional learning communities to emerge.

PROFESSIONAL LEARNING COMMUNITIES EMBODY CERTAIN DISPOSITIONS OF PRACTICE

Over the past eleven years, in our work at Communities for Learning, we have discovered that the teachers and administrators who were attracted to and wanted to be a part of our organization shared specific values, tendencies, and behaviors related to how they saw themselves, how they approached their work, and how they defined their roles and responsibilities.

Over time, and by testing our characterizations in different school, district, and regional contexts, we have been able to articulate what we see as six dispositions of practice that characterize individuals and organizations that are attracted and committed to professional learning communities. These dispositions represent, assess, and guide the work of individuals who participate in these communities and the organizational contexts that support that work. They influence how these individuals and communities see themselves, approach their work, and define their roles and responsibilities. They inform the kinds of interventions that can be designed to create the conditions for individuals and schools to begin to create professional learning communities. Finally, they provide the foundation for the norms and processes that communities engage in and support. We have defined them as dispositions because they represent abiding tendencies that reflect the values, commitments, practices, and professional ethics that influence behaviors and actions. Our definition of disposition is closest to Ritchhart (2001), who characterizes dispositions "not only as what one can do, one's abilities, but also what one is disposed to do. Thus, dispositions address the often noticed gap between our abilities and our actions." (p. 143).

These six dispositions are:

- Commitment to Understanding

- Intellectual Perseverance

- Courage and Initiative

- Commitment to Reflection

- Commitment to Expertise

- Collegiality

Commitment to Understanding refers to the commitment to thoughtfulness in the pursuit of questions and the development of ideas related to teaching and learning; the use of data, research, and evidence in work and argumentation; and the access and use of multiple perspectives. This disposition provides the community with the fodder for sound decision making and strategic planning by enabling it to identify and use the most relevant and pertinent data to improve or revise its thinking and practice and be able to adopt and use well-reasoned and sound school improvement structures. It supports the community and its members through the continuous use of data and of teacher and student work to improve teaching and learning. It provides the community with quality control mechanisms to uphold high standards and supports a reasoned and strategic process in considering changes and innovations to be adopted.

Intellectual Perseverance is the willingness to change and improve through the continuous revisiting of one's own work or the pursuit of ideas or questions for a period of time. It reflects a commitment to completing work to publicly held standards. It provides a professional learning community with patience and thoughtful behavior related to decisions and actions, all of which are central to having an explicit internal quality control process. Intellectual Perseverance supports professional learning communities and their participants by enabling them to produce quality work for adults and students, such as curriculum, instruction, and assessment, and by emphasizing revision processes that lead to high-quality and thoughtful behavior.

Courage and Initiative is a willingness to face new challenges, enter unchartered territory, and share work in unfamiliar ways or genres or with an unknown audience. As a disposition, it supports the professional learning community by promoting intellectual curiosity and innovative thinking. It is evident when individuals have the courage to pursue new roles and responsibilities and are open to change and innovation; when they make their values and assumptions explicit in the pursuit and discussion of uncomfortable topics; when they tolerate cognitive dissonance and conflicts that emerge from trying to reconcile and value competing perspectives or when they confront issues that have no clear resolution; and when they ask questions of each other that reveal their own ignorance. Courage and Initiative promotes a climate that engenders shared responsibility, the assumption of new roles, divergent thinking, and the development of novel ideas, products, and processes.

Commitment to Reflection is about devoting and valuing time to think, ask questions, consider current actions and work, evaluate activities and work, set goals, plan future actions, or make decisions that might improve their thinking and their work. Although all of the dispositions play an important role in the development of professional learning communities, Commitment to Reflection deepens all of the other dispositions by promoting thoughtfulness, deliberate planning and decision making, and responsive behaviors in the light of threats, changes, or conflicts.

Commitment to Expertise is about an active engagement in the identification, development, production, dissemination, and publication of professional knowledge and expertise. It supports the professional learning community by promoting knowledge generation, thereby legitimizing the wisdom of professional practice. It is evident when members of the community develop, exchange, and share their learning and expertise and when they search for disseminating and publishing avenues within and outside their place of work.

As a disposition of practice, Collegiality concerns an interest in and the pursuit of active learning with and from others; a willingness to share authority for learning and doing; drawing on each other's expertise to foster collaborative learning and problem solving; and the understanding that social learning is fundamental to the community and the individuals within it. Collegiality strengthens the professional learning community by creating the very conditions that support community and by promoting the creation and dissemination of distributed intelligence or expertise.

Although I have described these dispositions as if they are self-contained, they relate to and support one another. All of them are ultimately necessary for a professional learning community to thrive, but some relate more to the substance or focus of the work of the community, whereas others address the means through which the work is produced or the glue that holds the community together. Commitment to Understanding, for example, is very much about the use of data and other information that relate to the work of teaching and learning, whereas Collegiality is primarily about the nature of relationships that are fostered or valued and not as much about the focus of those relationships. It is as difficult to imagine Commitment to Understanding and Intellectual Perseverance in the absence of Commitment to Reflection, as it is to imagine Commitment to Expertise in the absence of Collegiality and Intellectual Perseverance.

It is entirely possible that other dispositions of practice play a role in supporting learning communities and that some of the dispositions I have identified embed other dispositions within them. For example, integrity is a disposition that supports but is separate from Intellectual Perseverance. Humility plays a key role in developing the trust that is needed to facilitate open and substantive discourse and is central to the pursuit of important questions related to practice. Although the work we have done to date underscores the importance of the six dispositions discussed in this chapter, we will undoubtedly continue to refine and expand our list as we work with new and different learning communities.

As with other tendencies and attitudes, we all have our strengths and weaknesses and have had different opportunities to develop ourselves and the communities in which we work. The dispositions of practice can become the focus of targeted interventions to support the development of individual and organizational readiness for learning communities and for the use of self-assessment and other evaluation tools. Developing them in individuals, schools, and learning communities can lead to the pursuit of worthy questions and goals about teaching and learning in contexts where such pursuit can be valued and sustained.

Developing Individual Capacity for Improving Schools

The ability of an individual or group to learn in a way that actually improves desired outcomes is constrained by several factors in complex systems—by limitations in the individual or collective knowledge base, by socially constructed belief systems, and by the very complexity of the interactions that define the organization.

J. O'Day (2004)

Developing the expertise and capacity of individuals to participate or support professional learning communities is intrinsically tied to the concept of readiness as a developmental construct. Every organization has individuals who are more or less ready to support professional learning communities. Readiness has many facets and components and involves skills, knowledge, and dispositions of practice. As compelling as the idea of working inside a community might be, not everyone is ready to embrace the idea or work of professional learning communities. Norms of isolation and privacy can be pervasive in schools and access to time for meaningful adult conversations scarce. The development of readiness to support professional learning communities begins with an understanding of where individuals are in terms of their awareness and perceived need for such a community. In schools and other organizations, this means that there has to be some awareness that the current reality is not all that there is or should be and that there are better possibilities.

The literature on professional learning, capacity building, and school improvement has identified many variables related to readiness (Hord, 2004; Louis and Kruse, 1995; King and Newmann, 2001; York-Barr and Duke, 2004; Lambert, 2005). Some readiness factors are structural; they have to do with the ways that activities or processes are organized, such as the way in which teachers are evaluated or the times that adults in schools can work together. Other readiness factors are dispositions of practice that reflect how individuals or groups are predisposed to behave or value. All of the components of readiness are necessary to initiate, sustain, or realize the full potential of professional learning communities. Without readiness, individuals cannot attend to the needs of the community or can sabotage the community with mandates, policies, or priorities that undermine its work.

Individual factors are knowledge, skills, and dispositions about teaching and learning, such as knowing how to create a classroom environment that facilitates student learning or being able to use meetings to assist the exchange of best practices among faculty. They include teacher and principal permanence, stability, and attrition, because it is hard to create trusting and stable relationships when people do not stay around long enough to build relationships. They involve engaging individuals who have credibility and approachability, leadership capacity, and a commitment to norms of shared practice and reflective thinking.

Louis and Kruse (1995) identified a willingness among individuals "to accept feedback and work toward improvement, a respect and trust among colleagues at the school and district level . . . and relatively intensive socialization processes" as readiness factors (p. 11). Much is lost when teachers are asked to engage in their own analysis of student work resulting from the implementation of literacy strategies but they lack the opportunity to learn from other teachers' experiences or from how other practitioners see their own and others' work. And providing teachers with times to meet and work without attending to structures and processes to maximize their time together does not make much sense.

How do we know that the people we want to invite to a professional community are ready to participate in it? What can we do to create the conditions that support a commitment to shared learning?

READINESS THROUGH THE DISPOSITIONS OF PRACTICE

Because the learning community is the environment in which the dispositions of practice defined in Chapter Two come to the forefront, individuals must have an interest in developing them in themselves and in their work in order to be willing and able participants in a professional learning community. Not everyone who volunteers for or is asked to be part of a professional learning community is aware of the value of these dispositions; nevertheless, they have the potential for developing them. Everyone possesses these dispositions to some degree and develops them at different rates, progressing along the four-point scale of beginning, developing, deepening, and embodying.

At the beginning level, individuals are aware of a disposition and may be interested in learning about it, but if the disposition manifests itself in the individual's learning or work, it is by happenstance. At the developing level, individuals may purposefully cultivate this disposition and it is possible to recognize it, albeit inconsistently, in some facets of their work. When they are at a deepening level, individuals actively pursue experiences to deepen their understanding and manifestation of a disposition. Finally, at the embodying level, they have internalized this disposition and integrated it into their lives and their work. They have also made it a focal point for self-assessment and goal setting. The beginning and developing levels speak more to readiness for participation in communities, and the deepening and embodying levels suggest a shift from readiness to capacity in the sense that individuals are now operating as full-fledged members of the professional learning community. The rubric in Appendix A depicts each of these levels.

In our work, we have found that when individuals join or agree to be part of a learning community, they come to it with at least a beginning level of readiness. They can take an active role in deepening their internalization of these dispositions. In many cases and over time, the professional learning community's processes and activities develop participants' readiness.

COMMITMENT TO UNDERSTANDING

When individuals demonstrate a readiness with respect to Commitment to Understanding, they articulate and pursue questions about their practice in general or about specific issues related to teaching and learning and read relevant material to increase their own learning. They may review their own students' work individually or with colleagues in order to ascertain their students' needs and allow others' perspectives to influence them, especially in situations where values come into question. This is illustrated when a group of teachers analyzes student work related to the implementation of specific teaching practices. Following is the reflection of a fourth-grade teacher, Mary Ellen Gamberg from Mattituck, Long Island, who, intent on helping students reflect on their understanding of poetry and accurately assess the strengths and weaknesses of their poems, explicitly attends to reconciling her desired goals with student data to rethink and revise future actions:

> When I reflected on the poems and technique reflections, as well as the final reflections that the students provided, I realized many things about my practice. It was clear that students were able to define and articulate many elements of writing poetry. To that end, my instruction met my expectation. However, when I reflected on what I actually wanted to see in their reflections, I realized that I did not execute the assignment in a way that would elicit those responses. The first error in judgment was to call it a posttest. As fourth graders, the word posttest promoted responses that mirrored test answers [rather] than reflective prompts. . . . It occurred to me that in the future, I should use two assessments: one as a way to demonstrate knowledge of poetic elements, and one as a reflection.

This reflection illustrates a deepening level of readiness in terms of Mary Ellen's use of relevant and pertinent data (see the "Deepening" column in Table 3.1).

In the absence of readiness for Commitment to Understanding, individuals ignore or dismiss questions about student learning, make general and unsubstantiated comments about the state of students' learning, negate others' perspective and interpretations of events and issues, and tend to be unaware of current

Table 3.1

Commitment to Understanding: Use of Research and Evidence

Beginning	Developing	Deepening	Embodying
Reaches conclusions about learning in the absence of specific evidence	Reviews work and data from a single source to ascertain students' learning needs	Uses work and data from several sources or measures to determine and discuss students' learning needs and identifies ideas for strategies to meet those needs	Uses multiple and different sources of data and other evidence to surface problems and issues or to test assumptions, hypotheses, and inferences related to learning

theories and best practices in education. An example of a lack of readiness is evident in the following scenario:

A group of teachers sits at a grade-level meeting complaining about the principal's refusal to accept discipline referrals and about what the group perceives are unreasonable demands by the school and the district. They make a number of complaints: "These kids are out of control." "The district is crazy to think that we can get them ready to pass the math test." "I am already behind, and it is only the first unit."

One teacher asks: "Doesn't he [the principal] understand that these children have no boundaries and are not ready to learn?" Another chimes in: "How many times have you had to remind the kids this week to bring their work?"

The principal describes himself as a manager and as the instrument of district policies and programs. When interviewed, he states that teachers should know what to do and how to teach since the district curriculum tells them what to do. He complains that the teachers lack classroom management skills and are skirting the responsibility of laying out clear expectations for student behavior.

The continuum of readiness and capacity related to Commitment to Understanding in terms of the pursuit of questions and the development of ideas related

Table 3.2

Commitment to Understanding: Articulation of Beliefs and Questions

Beginning	Developing	Deepening	Embodying
Repeats questions that others raise	Identifies and pursues others' questions to focus own inquiry	Raises and pursues own questions to increase learning and explore own and others' assumptions	Questions and raises issues that challenge the status quo and demand a reexamination of deeply held assumptions
Questions are numerous, general, or unfocused	Questions are specific to a topic but may not deepen understanding	Questions are focused and deepen understanding of a topic or lead to new questions	Questions target a gap in the current research on a specific topic and lead to new, pertinent questions

to teaching and learning is illustrated in Table 3.2. The behavior of both teachers and the principal suggests that they are still operating at a prereadiness level of the continuum.

The following questions may help individuals assess their readiness related to Commitment to Understanding:

• What role does inquiry play in decision making and in practices?

• What information or data inform my decisions about practices, policies, programs, or processes?

• How do I ensure that my conclusions are supported by multiple sources of data or by the right kind of evidence?

• How do I decide what data to use to inform my thinking and make decisions?

• How is information or data used and shared?

Individuals can increase their readiness in terms of Commitment to Understanding by accessing and using data that are related and relevant to their needs, seeking coaching and support on how to best use those data, exploring the use of baseline (diagnostic) and summative assessments to measure the impact of their interventions on students or others, and accessing others' perspectives on their understandings and decisions.

INTELLECTUAL PERSEVERANCE

Consider the following scenario.

Ms. Lin has been teaching fifth grade in the same school for twenty-seven years. She is proud of the fact that she can pull out any lesson she needs from her file cabinet and that she can access her entire curriculum through carefully labeled and color-coded folders. Her quizzes are filed in chronological order, from September through May, so she does not need to worry about creating new ones. Ms. Lin's classroom operates as if it were an efficient factory. There are clearly articulated rules and regulations. She complains repeatedly about the fact that students are not like they used to be: they do not pay attention to her, they are disrespectful, and they don't want to do what she tells them to do.

Ms. Lin's principal refers to her school as a good one that exhibits no problems and that has clearly delineated policies as to who does what, in what ways, and for what reasons. She does not mention anything related to teaching and learning. Ms. Lin and other teachers in the school have no ownership of any of the school policies and complain to one another about feeling oppressed by them. It is no surprise that their lack of ownership is exacerbated by the continuous exercise of blame.

When individuals are at a prereadiness level in Intellectual Perseverance, as are Ms. Lin and her principal, they claim to be disempowered about changing the current reality. They repeatedly rely on the same materials and resources regardless of changes in their student populations or in curricular demands, and they do not question their quality or the status quo, and they are unable to see how to makes changes in the school. They also see themselves as policy enforcers rather than professionals.

When individuals reach readiness, they discuss ideas for lessons, assessments, or other work with their colleagues and make note of needed revisions to their work, using time provided by the school or district to revise that work. They recognize the value of sharing and learning from each other and the importance

Table 3.3

Intellectual Perseverance: Commitment to Revise and Improve Own Work

Beginning	Developing	Deepening	Embodying
End product is virtually the same as the original draft	Identifies needed revisions to own work	Revises thinking and work to correct perceived problems	Rethinks or revises own thinking, producing multiple drafts of improved work
Uses time provided for revision to accomplish other tasks	Revises own thinking and work within time provided by those expecting the revisions	Finds or makes the time necessary to revise own thinking and work	Revises own thinking and work on a continuous basis, even when faced with impending deadlines or fatigue

of revising their work and their practice. Table 3.3 illustrates a continuum of readiness in terms of a commitment to revision.

A dialogue that ensues when teachers review student work to answer questions related to the impact of their practices on student learning demands readiness in terms of intellectual perseverance. The questions include:

- How might I modify the lesson or assignment to increase its effectiveness or impact?
- How can I adapt this lesson to address the needs of students who don't think that they can read, write, or problem solve?
- How can I modify the activities in this unit so that my least motivated students can participate and learn?

Other questions may assist individuals in examining themselves and their overall practice related to intellectual perseverance:

- In what ways do I exhibit flexibility and open-mindedness?
- How do I use feedback from others to improve my work?

- When someone challenges my thinking, how do I know I've moved from disagreement to rethinking my stance, and how do I reconcile conflicting perspectives?

- How do I know when it is time to walk away and take a step back, and how do I know when I am done and it's time for new goals and questions?

- What are the standards I use to evaluate my work, and how do I know I have met them?

The most natural path to increasing Intellectual Perseverance is to access models or examples from individuals or schools that depict the quality or performance standards we would like our own thinking and work to reflect.

COURAGE AND INITIATIVE

I recently visited a school in which all the fourth-grade students who scored below standards on a test administered in September that simulated the state test were separated from their peers for two hours each day during part of their language arts and social studies periods. During those two hours and for a period of two months, they were placed in a drill-and-practice program, rehearsing items that mirrored the state test. For weeks, teachers complained about increased behavioral problems with these students and about the fact that they were lagging behind in both their English and social studies work. Parents complained about struggling to get these students to school and about their increased defiance when they told them to do something at home.

When confronted by parents and teachers, the principal not only defended his remedial program but argued that this was the only sure way of accomplishing his goal of getting the school to comply with the district's expectations. Plagued by increasing complaints, the principal instituted a closed-door policy that made it almost impossible for anyone to approach him.

Courage and Initiative, as a disposition, is related to a sense of safety or security and is deeply affected by contextual issues since individuals are less likely to take risks if they don't feel that the ground on which they stand is safe. It involves raising or discussing uncomfortable topics or issues, including one's values and assumptions. It also relates to seeking or accepting new challenges or responsibilities and accepting the discomfort that stems from needing to change one's thinking or work.

When individuals like this principal are at a prereadiness level of Courage and Initiative, they ignore, avoid, or personalize issues or questions about teaching and learning. They hide or deny the existence of their own professional issues or questions from colleagues or others. They ignore dissenting points of view and shy away from discussions related to equity or any controversial or moral issue.

When individuals feel safe enough to take small risks and operate at a beginning level of readiness, they raise questions about their work, roles, or responsibilities. They participate in discussions around issues or questions about teaching and learning with the intent of finding an answer or coming to a resolution. They seek guidance from others who are like them in resolving issues or problems. They can participate in discussions initiated by someone other than themselves that may be uncomfortable, such as those around equity issues, and they may view situations in which there are divergent or conflicting needs as problems to be solved.

A continuum from readiness to capacity in terms of sharing their work and assuming new roles and responsibilities is represented in Table 3.4.

Increasing readiness to assume risks has much to do with revisiting one's vision, goals, and sense of purpose and juxtaposing them against the current

---

Table 3.4
Courage and Initiative: Sharing of Work in Unfamiliar Contexts, Ways, or Genres or Pursuing New Roles and Responsibilities

Beginning	Developing	Deepening	Embodying
Avoids sharing own work or thinking, or apologizes before sharing any work	Shares work and ideas but only after almost everyone else in the group has done so	Shares completed and unfinished work openly when opportunities are presented to do so	Shares work, ideas, and questions at any stage of development if doing so might lead to clarification, improvement, or resolution
Maintains current position or responsibilities even when they are not challenging	Accepts new roles or responsibilities but is hesitant and uncomfortable with this change	Seeks and accepts new responsibilities and is interested in learning from them	Actively seeks new challenges, roles, and responsibilities as a way of staying energized

reality and the choices that are made to support it. It also entails recognizing our responsibility and sense of agency in pursuing our goals and maintaining a strong sense of self. To assess their disposition of Courage and Initiative, individuals may ponder questions such as:

- Under what conditions do I take a risk?

- What do I gain when I do?

- What do I lose?

- What role does social discourse and discussion play in helping me find the answers to difficult questions or pursue the solution to problems?

- How do I handle my own ignorance, cognitive dissonance, conflict, controversy, and dissenting points of view?

- How do I make my assumptions explicit to myself and others, and which values and assumptions am I most likely to conceal or reveal?

- How do I challenge myself and others to consider alternative points of view?

- When do I assume new or unfamiliar roles and responsibilities?

COMMITMENT TO REFLECTION

Individuals who are lacking in this disposition operate and exist in the moment, viewing each event as separate and isolated from others, focusing on the work at hand, and seeing it as disconnected from future or past. Consider the following situation:

Mr. Harris has been implementing the new reading series that the district purchased. Central to the series are flexible groups or classroom centers, but Mr. Harris has no knowledge of either. So he "covers" the readings and writing assignments each day by asking students to do them, while ignoring any recommendations or proposed learning experiences that are new to him. His students are struggling with the readings and the assignments.

Mr. Harris blames the reading program and his school district for his students' problems. He believes that if the district is unwilling to buy a better reading program, it should at least provide him with a full-time reading aide.

Mr. Harris's behavior and perceptions characterize a prereadiness stage in a Commitment to Reflection through an exclusive focus on his own perspective and a refusal to speak about his own work, even though he has much to say about the work of others. His lack of readiness is also illustrated by his characterization of proposed innovations, in this case the reading program, as impossible or likely to fail and his complaint about needed improvements.

A beginning level of readiness is evident when individuals acknowledge a connection between their own work, their reality, and their self-understanding; when they articulate either broad and idealistic goals or narrow and disjointed goals related to needed actions; and when they identify areas for improvement and consider suggested actions in terms of how they relate to their work.

A developing level of readiness is evident in the following quotation by a teacher, Angela Fuller, who is a third-year member in a professional learning community:

> I've come a long way in the past three years. I feel I am a better teacher and my students are receiving a higher level of instruction, which is evident in their progress and learning. I continue to struggle with providing opportunities for student reflection. However, I now fully understand its importance. My assessments no longer consist solely of a chapter test. I work hard to create more opportunities for my students to demonstrate their knowledge. I've also come to realize the power of collaboration with other teachers in regards to analyzing student work.

Increasing our readiness to reflect has much to do with our willingness to devote time and energy to think about our decisions, learning, and work in ways that increase our thoughtfulness. Some of these questions may help individuals assess and improve their practice and their thinking in terms of their Commitment to Reflection:

- What formal opportunities in or outside my work do I have to be thoughtful about teaching and learning?

- How do I hold myself accountable for the time and thoughtfulness needed for purposeful and effective reflection?

- How do I intentionally use feedback from others to inform and refine my practice?

- What role do goal setting and action planning have in my work?
- How do I determine future actions and decisions?

COMMITMENT TO EXPERTISE

When teachers refuse to share their lessons, their assignments, and their students' work with each other; when the bulletin boards display little student-generated work and such work is not graded or responded to; when no one volunteers to guide a discussion of their peers or participate in a study group, even if participants can decide what to study; when teachers close their door as soon as students enter; or when unskilled administrators create unpleasant or embarrassing experiences in the name of "sharing our work," there is a strong indication that they are operating at a prereadiness level in terms of their commitment to developing and disseminating expertise. Individuals at this level are uninterested in professional learning or engaging in any kind of inquiry. They also avoid situations that might lead to developing or sharing professional knowledge or expertise.

At a beginning level of readiness, they recognize that they need to learn more, but they circumscribe that learning to predetermined time slots, like required professional development or department or grade-level meetings.

Consider the following situation:

Stemming from an alternative to the traditional teacher observations that are part of the formal evaluation process, a kindergarten teacher has completed a comprehensive year-long action research study around language development in early primary levels. At the end of the school year, she shares her findings and new questions at a grade-level faculty meeting. When asked if she is interested in sharing her insights at a regional literacy conference, she says, "I don't know enough about this to present at a conference."

Individuals who are at a developing level of readiness, as is the case of this teacher, engage in their own research around an area of personal interest. They are willing to share their learning, experiences, and expertise with colleagues and will consider requests to share learning at faculty, grade-level, or department

Table 3.5

Commitment to Expertise: Sharing and Disseminating Expertise

Beginning	Developing	Deepening	Embodying
Dreads the idea of presenting own work	Views presenting or sharing of own work as an obligation	Views presenting own work as a responsibility	Holds presenting at superintendent conferences or in other public forums as an expectation for own self, and not a perk or unusual privilege
Is hesitant to acknowledge learning, experiences, or expertise	Is willing to share learning, experiences, and expertise with peers	Is willing to share learning, experiences, and expertise with colleagues who share roles and responsibilities	Makes explicit efforts to share learning, experiences, and expertise with others within and beyond the individual's own work setting

meetings. But they are not yet willing to believe that their own expertise could be useful to others. Table 3.5 shows the continuum of readiness and capacity related to a commitment to dissemination.

One of the primary variables important to Commitment to Expertise relates to negotiating the fine line between effectiveness and expertise. Notwithstanding the role that participants serve in their organization (for example, teachers, principals, central office staff, professional developers, students, university professors, representatives of community-based groups of nongovernmental organizations) and the skills and knowledge that support the teaching and learning that they bring to the community, most participants in professional learning communities see themselves, first and foremost, as learners.

Expertise is a word that most students and practitioners in schools shy away from; it conveys a state of being rather than a state of becoming. As Strong (2007) has argued, what teachers and students know about teaching and learning is clearly tested on a daily basis, but few recognize it as legitimate knowledge.

Practitioners have no problem identifying their experiences or the kind of work they do and the questions that plague them. They have a much harder time using the word *expertise* as something they possess. A deep-seated legacy of egalitarian traditions, coupled by a strong labor union influence on the teaching profession, makes it problematic for teachers to assert their expertise publicly. Yet the very premise that participants in a learning community are agents of school improvement, who have a commitment to the development and dissemination of expertise, demands the public articulation of everyone's expertise.

Over eleven years ago, when we started the professional learning community at Communities for Learning, we sought to bridge the experience and expertise of its fellows by asking them to complete what we termed a *table of expertise*. Fellows included dedicated and thoughtful educators who spent an average of five years as fellows studying their own practice and reconciling their individual interests and passions with the vision and needs of the organizations for whom they worked.

Angela DiMichele Lalor, a middle school teacher in a Long Island, New York, school district who later became a professional developer, sought to deepen her vast experience as a social studies teacher by creating a standards-based curriculum unit that showcased a range of assessments and rubrics. Her work as a fellow later included an exploration of ways to assist special educators in incorporating state standards into their teaching practices.

Diana Muxworthy Feige, a faculty member at Adelphi University, in Garden City, New York, began her work as a fellow with a deep interest and commitment to student reflection and to bridging the distance between theory and practice. These interests translated into the development of various service learning opportunities and field-based work in schools for university students.

Shirley Glickman, a literacy coach in an elementary school in Bronx, New York, began her fellowship with a deep commitment to helping students succeed on state tests. She developed a protocol for teaching teachers how to coach students in the analysis of state test expectations and in the exploration of such expectations as evidenced in writing samples.

Table 3.6 shows an excerpt.

We discovered two things. First, fellows resisted the notion of identifying areas of expertise and wanted to replace it with "interested in" or "has worked on." Second, much of what they entered into that table said little about their own expertise. Instead, they identified work that they had studied or become adept at, using words that reduced such work to widely used but not very clearly defined labels, such as "action research" or "using data."

Table 3.6
Sample Table of Expertise

Communities for Learning Fellow	Curriculum and Assessment Design	Research and Inquiry	Reflective Practice
Angela DiMichele Lalor—middle school teacher Work: "My Personal Connection"	Standards-based social studies units Standards-based gap analysis Rubrics Special education Curriculum guides Academic Intervention Services	Supporting student writing Special education support strategies	Teacher and student portfolios Special education portfolios Documentation tools for curriculum alignment
Diana Feige— university professor Work: Action research on service learning		Systems thinking, especially the work of Gregory Bateson Mentoring student teachers Action research	Reflection as an essential component of student teaching Student portfolios
Shirley Glickman— Work: "How Does Classroom Assessment Practice Affect Student Writing?"	Language arts, grade 4: state assessment Rubrics Unit planning in reading and writing Nonfiction writing Designing curriculum calendars	Action research on the effectiveness of student rubrics and self-assessment Using data Literature circles	Student reflection Writing workshop

To support the fellows in clearly articulating their expertise, we studied the work of York-Barr and Duke (2004) and Shulman (2004) and provided them with various conceptions of expertise, such as the one held by Dreyfus and Dreyfus (1986), who identify five levels of expertise: novice, advanced beginner, competent performer, proficient performer, and expert. However, our most significant intervention with the Communities for Learning fellows was a brief presentation by Richard Strong, a national consultant who has devoted much of his career to helping teachers develop thoughtful classrooms. Strong helped them see that the questions and needs that we all have are part of our expertise. He shared with them his own list of "efficiencies and deficiencies" with items such as inventing routines for others to follow as an efficiency ("what I am good at") and following routines as a deficiency ("what I have trouble with and seek to avoid").

As a result of this work around helping fellows define their expertise, they are becoming much clearer about who they are and are more comfortable with what they bring to the community. They now are able to articulate their expertise around questions and topics they have had experience in pursuing and have deeper questions about. They are better able to share work related to the dispositions of practice they feel more accomplished in and are able to assist others who are working to develop those dispositions. They can delve into finding the substance behind the practicalities of teaching students or working with teachers and can see that substance as a reflection of their accomplishments. They can speak to areas in their work that they feel well versed in and can juxtapose them with areas in their work they are interested in talking about with others.

One of the Communities for Learning fellows, Mark Levine, a principal of an elementary school in the Bronx, New York, illustrates how we tend to view our own expertise in this way:

> Why do we balk at defining what we are most comfortable and competent doing as expertise? Humility? False modesty? The challenge in defining our own expertise may be in peeling away the doubt and appraising ourselves as others might see us, or as we may secretly want to see ourselves. It may also be that there are degrees of expertise, and we are reluctant to consider ourselves as experts because we don't always rise to what we might consider the highest level of expertise. It may be useful to look at our expertise on a continuum.

Following are two other illustrations; the first one, shown in Table 3.7, is from Liz Locatelli, a high school teacher and professional developer in Rockland County, New York, and the second one, shown in Figure 3.1, is from Tammy Pozantides, a special education and bilingual education specialist from Buffalo, New York.

Table 3.7
Liz Locatelli's List Defining Her Expertise

Things I Feel Good About	What I'd Like to Improve
I create assessments that clearly match the goals I want to address.	I would like to use these more consistently in my own teaching.
I can analyze data to determine where the students are and what they need; I can explain this clearly to others.	I would like to do this more automatically and consistently.
I can share what I know in small groups.	Sometimes I could listen better. I can get so caught up in the ideas evoked by the conversation that I miss what someone is saying or jump in too quickly.
I can give good constructive feedback to teachers and adjuncts, and I can show them ways to improve what they have written or planned.	I try to be sensitive, but I have to consider when I need to be more accepting of where the person is and to mitigate standards a bit until the person is ready.
I can take the ideas of a group and mesh them into a program, policy, or document.	I might be too quick to work things out. Taking more time to generate ideas might improve my thinking process.
I am good at designing and facilitating workshops and have done several on a variety of topics.	I tend to fizzle out at the end and to lose energy. I need to maintain a more even keel.

Questions that may assist individuals in thinking more deeply about their commitment to developing and disseminating expertise include:

- How do I view myself in terms of professional expertise?

- What role does continuous learning and inquiry play?

- What new skills and knowledge have I pursued to develop my expertise in a specific area?

- How do I work to develop and investigate existing knowledge of a subject?

- How do I share my expertise with others?

Figure 3.1
Tammy Pozantides's Reflection on Her Own Expertise Through an "Expertise Equalizer"

Areas of Expertise	Novice	Competent Performer	Expert
Content-focused and cognitive coaching	—	——	—————————
Developing schoolwide behavior plans	———————	———————
Communities for Learning	——	———————————
Facilitation skills	———————————————	———
Collaborative teaching	————————————	——————
RTI (response to intervention)	——	—————————————
Writing for publication	—	——————————————
Meeting the needs of diverse learners (bilingual, English language learner)	————————————————	—
Understanding native Spanish speakers language arts	——————	—————————

- How have I implemented job-embedded, collaborative professional models to further my own and others' learning and practice?

- In what ways, if any, do I have opportunities to share or disseminate what I know with others within and outside the school?

A commitment to develop and share what we know can be fostered by accepting the legitimacy of our own experience, seeking experiences to deepen and broaden our current understandings, and accessing informal and formal forums to exercise the responsibility of sharing and disseminating what we know and understand.

COLLEGIALITY

Let's examine an example of prereadiness:

Every school day, Mrs. Peters arrives at the school at 7:55 A.M. and leaves at 3:15 P.M. Her classroom materials and teaching files are stored and locked in a four-drawer file cabinet next to her desk. She is a fairly competent science teacher who keeps abreast of best practices through reading research and attending science courses at a local university. She is extremely shy, and her lack of interpersonal skills has served to isolate her from others. Over the past three years, she has not been part of any staff committee or task group. When asked to participate in any collaborative endeavor at grade-level or departmental meetings, she sits with her peers but focuses on her own work.

Individuals like Mrs. Peters operate at a prereadiness level. They attend only to their own needs and responsibilities, avoid conversations with colleagues, and operate as if they did not need, or could not benefit from, interaction with others.

At a beginning level of readiness, individuals share their work when someone asks them to, offer and accept support from others when required, and participate in collaborative work when invited to do so, but they focus exclusively on their own work.

An example of a developing level of readiness involves a group of administrators who are invited by their superintendent to engage in a study group around effective feedback to create common tools and processes for giving feedback to teachers. In the process of developing those tools, they share their approaches for responding to teachers' work.

Developing collegiality as a disposition begins with a recognition of the value of shared experiences to learn from and with others. To assess and consider their commitment to collegiality, individuals could pursue the following questions:

- What role does collaboration play in my work and in my school?

- Who do I collaborate with?

- To what end?

- How do I demonstrate interest in and active learning with others?

- What questions do I pose?

- How have I fostered discourse that invites members of a group to expand and build on one another's work or thinking?

- How have I worked with others to clearly articulate best practices, experiences, or knowledge so that others can benefit?

- In what way do I assist colleagues in a search for the implications of their work or thinking?

- How have I encouraged others to create and support positive changes in learning environments?

CONCLUSION

Ascertaining individual readiness for professional learning communities is an important step toward creating it. When readiness exists, the work of developing learning communities is much easier. However, individual readiness cannot be divorced from organizational readiness and the capacity of organizations to support the individuals who comprise them. Neither one of them operates in isolation of the other. Readiness and capacity include the acquisition and use of shared knowledge, skills, and dispositions, as well as the ability to create and develop the need for and the space for such knowledge, skills, and dispositions. Supporting the acquisition of individual knowledge, skills, and dispositions entails attending to the organizational capacity required to accept and embrace what individuals have to offer and providing an environment that supports rigorous discourse and inquiry related to teaching and learning.

Developing School and District Organizational Capacity

S chool programs, structures, policies, and practices tend to foster isolation rather than collaboration and integration, promoting, at best, individuals who pursue their own learning agendas without a shared purpose for their learning. A district whose policy related to professional development is to give every staff member money to attend a conference of his or her choice or to buy resources for his or her own learning may support the learning of individuals, but this is not a learning community.

From an organizational perspective, the development of professional learning communities is, first and foremost, about laying the groundwork for the acceptance of the work generated by individual capacity. It also includes realizing the importance of creating environments, such as cross-role groups, where practitioners of all kinds can pursue the work of learning communities without getting bogged down with the politics in their own work contexts or situations. In this way, the work and the learning of participants in the professional learning community can transcend the boundaries and limits of an individual, allowing attention to be paid to the overall focus of improving learning, rather than the individual issues and concerns of any given role.

A principal who is concerned with staff's commitment to a particular initiative can, on entering the professional learning community experience, shed that responsibility or share it, formally or informally, with other members of the community who may be focused on shared leadership, transforming the issue from its particularities, to one that is shared by the collective and used as a way of better understanding and grappling with issues of learning for all.

The conditions that support professional learning communities relate to the structures, roles and responsibilities, climate, and context of all organizations. Some of them are common to all the contexts in which learning communities can be found. Regardless of whether a learning community is housed in a school, a district, a university, or a region, the role of leadership and shared responsibility will be critical to creating and then sustaining the community. Nevertheless, a professional learning community in a school may require different actions and strategies from its members than would a district-based or a regional learning community. Similarly, the conditions that are required to form a community differ slightly once the community is formed. A community that has evolved and matured has a resilience that is lacking in one in which participants have yet to realize the purpose or value of their community.

Organizations that support learning communities assign roles and responsibilities to teachers and other community members based on their experience and expertise. They place high trust in the people in their organization, especially those who cultivate positive working relationships among peers, administrators, and others who have formal leadership positions. They offer tangible support to informal leaders who, despite the absence of formal leadership titles or roles, engage in the work of leading, and foster experiences that help everyone in the organization clarify and negotiate roles and responsibilities in ways that develop shared accountability. Such experiences might include peer coaching, mentoring, or facilitation work.

Such organizations create a climate that fosters a shared mission, vision, and purpose for student learning. As a result of their engagement in the collective identification and sharing of assumptions and practices related to teaching and learning, they foster site-based and participatory decision-making processes that deemphasize hierarchies and are used for problem finding, problem solving, decision making, scenario planning, and the production of work. They model reflective professional inquiry and provide administrative support for the community and its members. They create conditions that foster courage and initiative and flexibility among its members, and they provide access to times and spaces for thoughtful conversation.

In schools and districts, these conditions are evident when principals and central office staff offer opportunities for staff to influence the school's activities and policies and when they assign leadership work to teachers that is central to teaching and learning. Such work might include facilitating meetings, engaging in action research work and collegial inquiry. They are also evident when principals recognize the uneasiness that teachers and other practitioners experience when they are assigned leadership roles that transcend their title and job description. They are manifested when schools and districts incorporate time blocks in their daily, weekly, or monthly schedules to support inquiry, collaborative learning, and leading among teachers.

In their research on teacher leadership, York-Barr and Duke (2004) identified a number of empirically based conditions that support teacher leadership and relate to professional learning communities. In terms of school culture and context, they include a schoolwide focus on learning, inquiry, and reflective practice and a climate that promotes courage and initiative. The expectation exists that individuals will engage in collaborative decision making and work, as evidenced by the way the teachers in Sandra Dyers's school (see Chapter Two) approach sharing the results of the strategies they have implemented. There is a positive regard for teacher leaders and the presence of strong teacher communities that foster professionalism.

At the school level, the most critical of these factors is a school leader, typically a principal who believes in the concept of a professional learning community and wants to realize it in his or her school. This belief is enacted through the development and reexamination of a shared vision, mission, and common purpose among staff and a serious effort at cultivating leadership across the building. Research on the role of principals suggests that professional learning communities in schools are most suitable when principals routinely and consistently listen to teachers, help them evidence their knowledge about teaching and learning, and follow through on their promises and decisions (Moller and others, 2000).

Leadership capacity, as defined by Lambert (2005), is one of the key conditions that support professional learning communities. Schools that have low readiness for professional learning communities can also be characterized as having low leadership capacity. These schools tend to be principal-dependent places, where teachers work in isolation from each other and there is a pervasive culture of blame and an absence of discourse around teaching and learning. Such blame is evident when a principal relies exclusively on test scores to determine the effectiveness of teachers or when a teacher determines that all the students' deficits can be traced back to a lack of parental involvement.

Shared leadership is about engaging in practices together and assuming a collective responsibility for student learning and for the school's well-being. It is key to professional learning communities. Principals who create a climate that supports shared leadership help teachers and other practitioners assert their role as professionals and, in some cases, as intellectuals. To do this, principals need to help others navigate what Little (2003) defines as "contested ground" for teachers—those conflicts that arise when teachers engage in professional practices such as designing innovative assessment mechanisms or creating coteaching approaches that clash with the bureaucratic language of school or district policies and constraints of the school's schedule.

The importance of the shared and collaborative nature of the work of professional learning communities cannot be overemphasized. DuFour, Eaker, and DuFour (2005) characterize collaborative work as a critical indicator of school readiness for learning communities, since it is geared toward improving the learning of students. Collaboration can improve learning for everyone, especially if it is mediated by processes that deepen discourse.

THE DISPOSITIONS OF PRACTICE IN ORGANIZATIONS

The organizational conditions that underlie structures, processes, and climates also underlie the development of the dispositions of practice of the professional learning community and its members. Just like individuals, organizations possess the dispositions of practice introduced in Chapter Two in different degrees. These can be measured along a continuum: beginning, developing, deepening, and systemic levels. At a beginning level, the organization may show evidence of the dispositions, but that evidence is purely inadvertent and not the result of purposeful attempts to understand or develop them. At a developing level, the dispositions can be recognized in different facets of the organization's work, but inconsistently. At a deepening level, the organization recognizes the importance of these dispositions and pursues experiences to deepen its understanding and manifestation in all aspects of the organization. At the systemic level, the dispositions are embodied and integrated into all levels of the organization and its work, providing a focal point for the organization's self-assessment and goal setting. The rubric depicting the progression from readiness to capacity at the organizational level is in Appendix B. The possibility that professional learning communities can be established or sustained is highly dependent on the creation of conditions that support these dispositions, including the use of specific interventions to establish the community and promote its development.

COMMITMENT TO UNDERSTANDING

From an organizational standpoint, commitment to understanding refers to supporting the pursuit of questions and development of ideas related to teaching and learning. This occurs through the access and use of multiple perspectives and data sources and research to identify and use the most relevant and pertinent data. Commitment to Understanding also concerns the adoption and use of structures such as design teams or collaborative decision-making groups aimed at improving teaching and learning for all members of the organization.

The readiness-capacity continuum as it relates to the use of multiple perspectives is depicted in Table 4.1.

Table 4.1
Commitment to Understanding: Use of Multiple Perspectives

Beginning	Developing	Deepening	Systemic
Consult selected individuals about decisions related to teaching, learning, and organizational development	Involve groups of selected individuals in discussions about teaching, learning, and organizational development	Engage mixed staff groups in conversations around teaching, learning, and organizational development	Use horizontal and vertical teams to uncover different perspectives and address questions about teaching, learning, and organizational development, especially related to whether organizational outcomes are as good as they can be

---

A school, a district, or a university at a readiness level related to commitment to understanding has a data collection system in place, though there may not be regular conversations about what the data reveal about student learning. In that school, the analysis of the data collected or available is superficial or not linked to any decisions about teaching and learning. The organization uses state or other standardized measures to determine the learning needs of its students and make related program or placement decisions. It provides opportunities for selected staff to engage in discussions around research-based practices and issues around curriculum, instruction, and assessment, possibly through their participation in committees or task groups. It responds to issues as they arise, such as proposing hiring new teachers in English as a Second Language instruction because of increasing numbers of incoming students from countries that have little formal education in their own language or in English.

The following agenda items for faculty meetings, used by a school principal to guide grade-level discussions with all staff over three months, illustrate a readiness level in terms of commitment to understanding:

1. Curriculum coherence: Where does the school have it? Where is it missing?

2. Use of data from different sources: What data are we using? From what sources? Who is using the information? For what purposes? How are the data informing our perceptions and decisions?

When a school lacks readiness in terms of commitment to understanding, it lets textbooks and other available resources determine its curriculum and assessment practices. It collects and uses data haphazardly and makes decisions about students' needs, placements, and programs arbitrarily and without referring to any data. It operates without any regard or access to research on best practices and is ever seeking to align school-related problems with new programs and initiatives. Finally, it lacks a specific structure or process for improving as an organization.

Where might we begin to intervene if we want to increase the school's readiness for professional learning communities as it relates to commitment to understanding? A starting place may be the creation of some dissonance among teachers around the relationship between their practices and student learning by asking questions such as these:

- What aspects of student learning and behavior do you control?

- What would you consider best practices when it comes to teaching your own children?

- What have you done to create boundaries that students can understand?

- What are the implications of your seeing yourself as not having control over the situation in terms of your work?

Engaging teachers in the review and discussion of articles about teaching and learning, followed by guiding questions that relate such texts to their practice, might be another starting point, especially if combined with opportunities for teachers to identify specific activities or strategies they could implement as a result of their reading and discussions.

District staff or outside agencies could increase the school or district capacity in terms of commitment to understanding in schools by helping principals form and join one or more teams to identify and study school-related problems such as discipline policies; examine ways in which student data on such topics as attendance, attrition, and referrals are used or ignored; or assess the merits of its programs and textbooks. Initially such teams might be limited in scope and operate during the free existing spaces for learning or problem solving, such as a superintendent conference day or as part of the annual state-mandated school review process. Later, and as a means to deepen readiness, as principals become more comfortable with expanding the purview of their responsibilities and with having input from staff, such structures could be expanded to and embedded in the ongoing work of the school so as to provide teachers and others with structured time and places for learning, problem solving, decision making, and designing activities.

Let's assume that a district lacks readiness in terms of Commitment to Understanding, and that this is manifested in the ways in which it uses student and other data to make decisions about students' needs and teachers' practices. Specific interventions that would move the district along the continuum from readiness to capacity include these steps:

1. Introducing central office staff to the notion of root causes and action planning based on identified needs

2. Engaging a committee that includes the superintendent and other administrators in the review of recent attendance data and test scores

3. Engaging a team comprising teachers and administrators in the examination of five-year trend data with groups to identify major problems or needs

4. Replicating the analysis of trend data with teachers and administrators from the entire district during a conference day or other professional development program while at the same time identifying additional data sources, including teacher and student work, to complement this analysis

5. Creating a structured time at least twice each year for the systematic analysis of trend data stemming from standardized tests and other internal measures to ascertain student needs and reconcile them with existing programs and policies

Questions that may help organizations think about themselves and their practices in terms of commitment to understanding include:

- What information or data inform our decisions about practices, policies, programs, or processes?

- How do we ensure that our conclusions are supported by multiple sources of data?

- How do we decide on what data to use to inform our thinking and make decisions?

- How are information or data used and shared?

- What role does inquiry play in our decision making and our practices?

INTELLECTUAL PERSEVERANCE

Intellectual Perseverance is the willingness on the part of the organizational leadership to discuss and revisit work and thinking in order to improve it, use vision and goals as a means of developing and assessing the organization, and establish and implement quality control mechanisms. The continuum of readiness to capacity in terms of a commitment to high standards is depicted in Table 4.2.

A school that exhibits organizational readiness in this disposition identifies a vision, often with the input of others, and publicly shares it. It announces several goals, related or unrelated, and asks staff to think of ways to support them, periodically requiring updates and information on the extent to which these goals and

Table 4.2

Intellectual Perseverance: Commitment to High Standards

Beginning	Developing	Deepening	Systemic
Recognizes that more time is needed to accomplish specific goals, but does not provide it	Stretches or bends deadlines if requested and needed to accommodate goal demands	Provides time necessary to accomplish goals at a desired level of quality	Anticipates the need for and builds in time to support achievement of goals and highest standards for work
Engages in immediate, full-scale implementation of initiatives	Moves from recommendations to large-scale implementation	Researches thoroughly before large-scale implementation	Routinely field-tests before piloting and pilots before large-scale implementation

priorities are being met. It also forms committees, identifying selected staff to investigate the organization's programs, practices, policies, or issues, and providing them with opportunities and time to ponder these efforts at organizational improvement.

An example of a school that operates at a developing level on the readiness continuum has engaged staff members in the development of a vision and mission that underscores the value of addressing the needs of all kinds of learners. It also has established goals related to teachers' use of differentiated instruction, learning about multiple intelligences and learning styles, and implementing a test-preparation program in mathematics in grades 4 and 8. It has sought the endorsement and support from selected faculty by engaging them in committee-related work around these goals.

A district with a low level of intellectual perseverance operates in the present, without a guiding vision for school improvement and without reference to explicit goals. The assumption is that everyone knows what they are doing and why, and there is no need to consider the organization's improvement or provide any professional development. In such districts, the administration tends to maintain tight control over all initiatives and strives to hold on to the status quo. Creating district policies without consulting staff fuels the kinds of attitudes displayed by some teachers who believe they have little or no control over what they can do to affect students.

Lack of readiness is also evident when task groups or committees explore ways of addressing the needs of the different populations of students and staff, but move directly from recommendations to large-scale implementation of ideas, projects, or policies instead of doing piloting or field-testing. They may implement new programs without much regard for consequences, intended and unintended. They may even buy programs or hire consultants to do work without considering the implications or effects of such innovations on processes, policies, or practices.

One of the beginning steps for creating readiness in Intellectual Perseverance is engaging the faculty and administration in visioning activities focused on describing the kinds of learners they want to produce and the kinds of teaching that will lead to desired student outcomes. Such a visioning process may need to be combined with support for the identification of clearly articulated, reasoned, measurable, and attainable goals. Another strategy revolves around reviewing and analyzing the demands imposed by state or content standards and exploring the ways in which current practices address those demands. This could be followed by the identification and the monitoring of curriculum, instruction, and assessment strategies to address student needs related to such demands. The idea behind these interventions is to create the space and time for review, analysis, and revision processes that are critical to the disposition of Intellectual Perseverance.

Questions that may assist schools and districts in thinking in terms of Intellectual Perseverance include:

- In what ways does our organization push itself and others to learn and grow?

- How are innovations implemented and monitored in our organization?

- How does our organization support staff work with colleagues and others to rethink, evaluate, and improve on knowledge and practice?

- How do we operationalize success?

- In what ways does our organization involve staff in its vision, goals, and initiatives?

COURAGE AND INITIATIVE

In organizations, courage and initiative concerns the openness to enabling the consideration and discussion of uncomfortable topics or issues, accepting the discomfort that stems from the need to change, and embracing challenges and

Table 4.3
Courage and Initiative: Openness to Innovation and Change

Beginning	Developing	Deepening	Systemic
Innovations are permitted as long as they do not require organizational resources or cause complaints from within or outside the organization	Innovations are supported as long as they do not deviate too far from what is accepted or expected and accomplish something that the organization perceives is needed	Innovation around educational questions or needs is encouraged, and resources are provided to support that work	Promoting innovative spirit is an organizational commitment supported by dedicated time, space, and resources
A process is in place for monitoring reactions to implemented organizational changes	Systems in place for gathering feedback related to proposed organizational innovations	Opportunities created for shared conversations around organizational issues or questions	Supports a culture and climate that allow innovation at all levels of the organization

innovations. The continuum of readiness to capacity in terms of embracing challenges and innovations is depicted in Table 4.3.

Schools that exhibit readiness in Courage and Initiative provide opportunities for discussions of shared questions, as well as for the exploration of conflicts and problems that arise. This was the case in the scenario in Chapter Three related to graduation requirements. These organizations value individuals whose views represent perspectives that are similar but not necessarily identical to those held by many and acknowledge the importance of situations involving the reconciliation of divergent or conflicting need. They support innovations, such as the possibility of reviewing and perhaps making changes to the fulfillment of graduation requirements, provided they do not deviate too far from what is accepted or expected. They also request and welcome feedback about the merits or implementation of such innovations.

A district with low levels of Courage and Initiative rewards maintenance of the status quo or imposes negative consequences on anything that does not produce immediate and predictable results, such as improving test scores. For example, it may offer merit pay exclusively on the basis of test results. It discourages innovation, expecting compliance with decisions made at an organizational level. Finally, it creates structures or processes that prevent questions that threaten established practices from being voiced, such as resolving the inequities produced by rigid tracking. This may be evident in the absence of clearly articulated policies or in the exercise of acts such as firing staff on the basis of questionable criteria.

Interventions to increase organizational readiness in such a district may include cognitive coaching practices and the careful introduction of single and small innovations that can increase support or resources for the leadership.

The kinds of interventions that could move any organization along a continuum of readiness to capacity would vary depending on the level of readiness of the organization. For example, in a school or district operated by a single leader who operated in an autocratic fashion, an initial intervention may entail identifying one or more individuals in the organization who share many of the beliefs and values of the formal leader but could share in the responsibilities of launching or managing specific innovations. This would result in the incipient formation of a leadership team.

Another intervention for a school lacking readiness in Courage and Initiative entails the implementation of an isolated innovation in an area that maintains or increases current resources or secures positive public support, as might be the case of adding a course offering or a paid after-school program. The success of such innovation might result in an increased willingness on the part of the school's leadership to consider other, less safe innovations.

Not having a formal leadership structure that values Courage and Initiative is one reason for a lack of readiness. Other reasons may have to do with prevailing cultural norms and mores or with the ways in which resources are allocated.

Depending on the factors that hinder Courage and Initiative, an organization might consider interventions such as conflict management and resolution strategies, developing norms for risk taking for the leadership and staff members, developing mechanisms for soliciting feedback on the merits of current initiatives and innovations, or instituting new ways for staff to provide their ideas and thoughts on new or existing programs or initiatives.

Once organizations have developed a readiness to support Courage and Initiative, they can concentrate on developing robust leadership teams, preferably comprising individuals with different roles within the organization, and on creating niches or silos for innovation and Courage and Initiative within the organization.

Some of the questions that organizations can use to determine their stance related to Courage and Initiative include:

- How open are we to considering changes in our organizational structures, programs, policies, and practices?

- How are Courage and Initiative manifested in our organization?

- Who takes risks?

- What role do social discourse and discussion play in helping us find the answers to difficult questions or pursue the solution to problems?

- How do we handle cognitive dissonance, conflict, controversy, and dissenting points of view?

- How do we make our assumptions explicit to others, and which values and assumptions are we most likely to conceal or reveal?

- How do we challenge others to consider alternative points of view?

COMMITMENT TO REFLECTION

In organizations, Commitment to Reflection is evident through a value for shared thinking as a way to develop and evaluate the organization, as well as support for self-assessment, monitoring, and strategic thinking processes, and the production of work that results from goals, actions, and strategies grounded in the analysis of past learning.

Schools, districts, and universities that exhibit readiness in Commitment to Reflection have a contractual language, policies, and programs that support reflective practice. Their staff members have at least some opportunities to reflect on their work and practice, as would be the case during pre- and postobservation interviews or during an annual goal-setting process. Supervisory staff members have time for the descriptive assessment of individuals who are evaluated and incorporate feedback from formative assessments before a formal staff evaluation is completed. The end-of year-review processes often include information about the degree to which individuals have worked toward or achieved institution-wide goals.

When a school, district, or university lacks readiness in Commitment to Reflection, it limits access to learning and professional development opportunities for staff by preventing them from attending or participating in workshops, study groups, and conferences. It also disregards staff members' engagement with self-selected learning opportunities and limits their ability to use or share what they have learned. In these organizations, the evaluation process, if it exists, is inconsistent and used primarily to provide a paper trail. It is primarily made up of a formal assessment of professional practices with a checklist that results in an overall letter rating. The appraisal of individual staff members' goal attainment may be done informally, inconsistently, and without a perceived need to encourage reflection or to tie the evaluation process to any goals.

Some of the interventions that might increase a school's readiness related to staff evaluation include soliciting the thoughts and comments of staff on the evaluation process components, sharing and discussing different models and processes, and ultimately involving staff members in the process of defining criteria and measures for their own evaluation.

Among the interventions that may increase organizational readiness are the use of reflective prompts in meetings and workshops, the modeling of reflection in decision-making or problem-solving situations, and the creation of formal opportunities for staff to think about, reflect on, and evaluate work they have accomplished, student needs, and organizational priorities. These interventions can be implemented by individuals within the organization or by outside facilitators. Overall, the most telling sign of lack of readiness in Commitment to Reflection is the absence of time or space for thoughtfulness.

The continuum of readiness to capacity in the area of supporting self-assessment, monitoring, and strategic thinking processes is depicted in Table 4.4.

Questions that organizations can ponder to assess their readiness in terms of Commitment to Reflection include:

- How do we set, monitor, and evaluate goals?

- What comprises the staff evaluation process?

- What does it measure? From whom do we seek feedback, and how do we use what we have learned?

- How does our organization give feedback? To whom does it give feedback?

- What is that feedback about?

- Perhaps most important, how does our organization promote thoughtful behaviors?

Table 4.4

Commitment to Reflection: Valuing Time for Thinking, Planning, and Self-Evaluation

Beginning	Developing	Deepening	Systemic
Verbally acknowledges importance of reflection, but does not provide opportunities for staff to display it	Provides opportunities for members of the organization to think about and ask questions related to needs	Engages staff members in opportunities to articulate and discuss thinking	Incorporates opportunities for staff to ponder and discuss questions and goals
Assumes that reflective practice or thinking is either an event or the responsibility of an individual	Provides selected staff with opportunities to reflect on their work and practice	Has a structure and processes in place to encourage reflective thinking	Establishes strategic structures and processes that encourage reflective thinking and practice, and periodically evaluates them
Expects staff evaluation reports to be completed on time	Expects adequate time to be provided for descriptive evaluation of staff	Communicates the need for staff to be provided with time for self- and peer evaluation based on work-related data provided	Creates opportunities for staff to self- and peer-evaluate and set prioritized goals based on the analysis of work-related data

COMMITMENT TO EXPERTISE

This commitment is evident in the organization's interest in refining and expanding current knowledge and skills, disseminating knowledge and expertise within and outside the organization, and supporting learning and work that address organizational or professional needs.

Schools and districts at a readiness level for Commitment to Expertise encourage their staff members to engage in self-selected learning opportunities and professional development and commend those who acquire additional certifications or credentials or publish their work. They may, for example, institute alternative professional evaluation mechanisms involving collegial learning or action research. They may rely on outside consultants to deliver professional development, but they also consider how to maximize the number of people exposed by expecting that those who participate will share and implement what is presented. If a team of teachers is sent to a regional professional development program, they would assume that on their return, the team would put into practice what they have learned and teach others to do so as well. These organizations consider requests from staff to share learning at specific organizational meetings like faculty, departmental, or grade-level meetings and provide opportunities for its own materials, products, and processes to be shared internally for comment and implementation. They allow connections with those in local universities or other educational organizations (such as having undergraduate students carry out their student teaching in the school or providing rooms for graduate education classes), provided there is adequate remuneration for the school.

When schools or districts lack readiness in the Commitment to Expertise, they disregard the knowledge, accomplishments, and work of their own staff. They are unconcerned with developing their staff's expertise or with disseminating any learning generated in the organization, and they avoid interactions with universities or other educational organizations. When faced with financial constraints, they cut funding for professional development first. They minimize or extinguish any formal opportunity for teachers or other staff members to share their accomplishments or newly acquired knowledge, and they establish policies that emphasize uniformity.

The continuum of readiness to capacity in terms of organizational interest in the dissemination of knowledge and expertise within and outside the organization is depicted in Table 4.5.

One of the strategies to increase individual readiness in this area is to ask staff about their areas of expertise, compiling their responses, and sharing them at a subsequent staff meeting with the intent of ultimately brokering relationships between people who have specific needs and others who have the capacity to address them. Another strategy includes asking every staff member to identify one or more learning goals and including the monitoring of those goals in annual professional evaluation reviews, provided this would be an acceptable practice in terms of the staff contract.

Table 4.5

Commitment to Expertise: Interest in Staff Members' Learning

Beginning	Developing	Deepening	Systemic
Requires staff to engage in predetermined learning or professional development	Encourages staff members to engage in self-selected learning and professional development	Expects all staff to think about their learning and work, and identify and pursue learning goals	Provides structured opportunities to, for example, develop learning, work, and questions; engage in research; and create professional portfolios
Believes professional development is a series of self-contained events	Expects professional development to result in staff able to implement their new learning	Considers professional development an opportunity for creating trainers	Treats professional development as an ongoing process to maximize expertise, effectiveness, and efficiency

To cultivate a Commitment to Expertise in schools, principals and other leadership staff could be invited to a conference or workshop on adult learning or job-embedded staff development; or they may be given literature on teachers teaching teachers, the relationship between well-prepared teachers and student outcomes, or comparative short- and long-term costs of curriculum that is scripted in ways that assume little if any need for judgment on the part of teachers vis-à-vis professional development that increases teachers' capacity. School and district staff could also be encouraged to begin an exploration of how to best induct and mentor new teachers or capture the expertise and experiences of faculty who are near retirement.

Questions that may assist organizations in thinking more deeply about their commitment to expertise include:

- How do we view the members of this organization in terms of professional expertise?

- What role does continuous learning and inquiry play?

- What new skills and knowledge has our organization pursued to enhance our expertise in a specific area?

- How do we work to develop and investigate existing knowledge of a subject?

- How do we share our expertise with others?

- How have we implemented job-embedded, collaborative professional models to further staff learning and practice?

- In what ways, if any, do we have opportunities to share or disseminate what we know with others within and outside our organization?

COLLEGIALITY

Collegiality manifests itself as an interest, from the organizational standpoint, in supporting learning with and from others, acting on the belief that learning and working with others increases expertise, and producing work that stems from collaborative learning and problem solving. This interest transcends the congenial climate of many schools, often involving food in the context of celebrating birthdays or other holidays. Collegiality is evident when people genuinely and actively seek to learn with and from others.

The readiness to capacity continuum in terms of acting on the belief that learning and working with others increases our expertise is depicted in Table 4.6.

Schools that are at a readiness level engage groups of teachers in addressing the needs of specific students or adults either by sharing what they know about those students or brainstorming ways of addressing specific needs. They encourage selected faculty or staff to expand their understanding of particular concepts or practices such as collaborative planning, cofacilitation, interdisciplinary curriculum design, and grade-level projects, and are willing to develop and share individual staff members' work and learning among their own staff or with selected practitioners from other schools or educational organizations. They may even seriously entertain proposals for collaborative structures and projects and form committees of administrators and other educators to accomplish necessary work related to them.

Schools lack readiness in terms of collegiality disavow the need for professional development experiences for their staff. They operate as if individual staff members already know what they need to know or can find what they need to know on their own. Executive decisions are made without consulting staff members who could be affected. In these organizations, there is a persistent belief that time to collaborate is just time for a cup of coffee. Consequently,

Table 4.6
Collegiality: Fostering Collaborative
Learning and Problem Solving

Beginning	Developing	Deepening	Systemic
Calls on a core group of staff members whenever necessary	Forms committees of like-minded individuals to accomplish necessary work	Forms committees that include diverse roles to accomplish necessary work or research	Brokers different kinds of relationships among staff to help everyone learn from others by organizing and using varied groupings (by role, responsibility, client, or interest)
Acknowledges the need for communication and collaboration	Considers proposals for collaborative structures and projects	Supports team configurations, common planning time, and visitations within the organization	Promotes activities such as peer coaching and explores different ways of accessing members' expertise and work

faculty and other staff rely on their individual judgment to make decisions about student needs.

Different types of interventions are needed to foster Collegiality depending on how much support an organization requires. For example, in an organization with little firsthand experience with collaboration, using efficiency as a lever to introduce scheduled collaborations between the formal leader and another individual or among a small group of staff members might be a good starting point. In organizations that have prior experience with information or have engaged in ad hoc collaborative practices, it may be better to introduce staff to cofacilitation and design approaches and, depending on their response, to experiences such as collaborative lesson study or integrated curriculum design. In settings where the formal leadership has not promoted much teamwork, appropriate interventions might include awareness experiences with shared leadership approaches or with the concept of distributed expertise, or even dialogues with staff in other organizations where collaborations are commonplace.

Some of the questions that may assist organizations in ascertaining their collegiality are:

- To what extent do we value collegiality and collaboration?

- What structures and systems do we have that promote collegiality?

- Who collaborates, and for what purposes?

- What role do collaboration and collegiality play in supporting our organization?

- What data can we collect on products or processes to show the effect of collaborative structures on our effectiveness or efficiency?

HOW STABLE ARE THE ORGANIZATIONS IN WHICH READINESS FOR PROFESSIONAL LEARNING COMMUNITIES HAS BEEN DEVELOPED?

Developing organizational readiness for professional learning communities would be far simpler if organizations were not complex systems that are affected by other systems and forces within and around them. Many of us have encountered contexts in which there is an imbalance between individual and organizational capacity. For example, some schools may have an organizational team that functions either within the school itself or at the district level and evidences a greater degree of readiness for professional learning communities than many of the individuals in that school or district. In other schools, changes in administrative staff may result in a setting in which the individuals within the school appear to exhibit a greater readiness for professional learning communities than is manifested by the organization. Figure 4.1 shows a graphic representation of different imbalances.

The initial readiness for professional learning communities is greatly affected by contexts that support it. If creating such readiness is an important goal, the first step toward its realization is to engage multiple stakeholders in a careful study of their school or organizational setting. The second step is to jointly identify multiple entry points for the development of such readiness in order to begin the work of professional learning communities. Engaging multiple stakeholders who care about the organization and its outcomes is critical because there is no magic list of entry points or interventions.

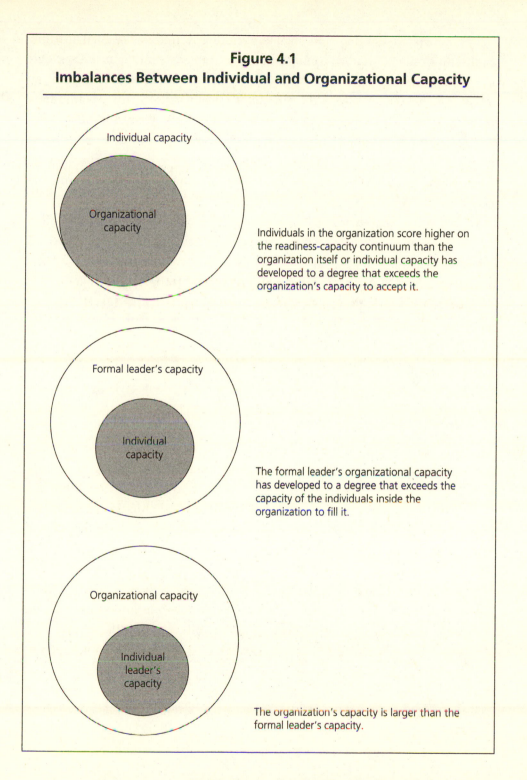

Figure 4.1
Imbalances Between Individual and Organizational Capacity

Individual capacity

Organizational capacity

Individuals in the organization score higher on the readiness-capacity continuum than the organization itself or individual capacity has developed to a degree that exceeds the organization's capacity to accept it.

Formal leader's capacity

Individual capacity

The formal leader's organizational capacity has developed to a degree that exceeds the capacity of the individuals inside the organization to fill it.

Organizational capacity

Individual leader's capacity

The organization's capacity is larger than the formal leader's capacity.

The efforts to develop and maintain readiness for professional learning communities might entail visioning and other strategic planning processes. One of the processes we have used begins with asking individual members of an organization who are vested in the concept of a professional learning community to consider the place in their organization in which they want to make a difference. They then imagine the place ten years from now and describe it using questions such as: What will it be like? Who will be there? What will be happening? What will be important? How will people behave? How will it be different from what is today? What will we see more or less of?

To develop a shared vision, they later engage in conversations with other individuals who share their roles or may be affected by their individual visions. Processes like this may provide individuals and learning communities with a shared sense of purpose as they engage in the work of facilitating, managing, and sustaining professional learning communities.

Facilitating, Assessing, and Sustaining Professional Learning Communities

The aim of education should be to enable individuals to learn with and from others. In a manner of speaking, the work of a professional learning community is to design and distribute thoughtfulness. It is about creating conditions where individuals can make the familiar and mundane strange enough so that it deserves further scrutiny. It is about extracting the inherent wisdom of grounded and well-reasoned practice. It is about teasing out the profound from the insignificant and about harvesting those rare moments in which one word, one action at the right time and place and with the right individuals, can become a strategy for tackling specific problems. The work of professional learning communities is as varied as its membership. To better understand it requires exploring the context that enables the work to be identified and negotiated, the forms that such work assumes, the roles that the facilitator and the participants play in developing it, and the processes that support its development, implementation, and sustainability.

CONTEXT THAT SURROUNDS THE WORK OF PROFESSIONAL LEARNING COMMUNITIES

The ultimate success of a professional learning community lies in its ability to define its purpose, its criteria for membership, and the values and norms it upholds. To enable participants to produce work that is valuable and valued, the professional learning community upholds key assumptions. First, it assumes that knowledge is socially constructed and that expertise is evident in the work of its participants, encouraging its members to test what they know and pursue what they don't know, individually and with others. It supports the framing of individual participants' understanding and the exploration of new areas of inquiry, deepens their areas of expertise, and helps them package and disseminate their work. The professional learning community provides and structures opportunities for its members to engage in deep conversations and inquiry around significant problems, issues, and ideas. It cultivates and embodies the dispositions of practice we have explored in previous chapters and holds all members accountable for what they know and for what they are trying to understand.

Defining the Community's Purpose and Focus

Once an organization has assessed its readiness to support professional learning communities, someone from within or outside the organization needs to define or help the community define its overall purpose. Determining whether the community is going to focus on learning, leading, or lasting is of primary importance because the expectations and support from the organization are very different for these three communities.

Sometimes the stated purpose of a professional learning community sheds some light regarding its membership, activities, and even its potential sustainability. For example, a community that is launched to solve a specific problem or accomplish a particular task is very different from one whose purpose is to improve the learning and work of all members of a community.

Over time, and sometimes regardless of their initial purpose, communities that learn can become communities that lead, and even communities that last. Certainly many communities have the inherent desire to see themselves as lasting, but such evolution is greatly dependent on the organization's commitment to the community, the facilitators' skills, and the participants' vision of themselves and of their community. The rubrics presented in Appendixes D, E, and F provide an overview of the three types of communities and how their purpose, focus, and membership can evolve.

Regardless of the specific situations that lead to the creation of a professional learning community, it is important to define the community's purpose and focus. Such definition can also happen before the community is formed or can be negotiated with community members. Exhibit 5.1 provides a checklist of criteria that can help inform the identification of the community's primary purpose.

Exhibit 5.1
What Is the Focus of My Learning Community?

Learning: Select no more than five of these.

❑ Connected to participants' backgrounds, interests, and needs.

❑ Supports the bigger picture of student learning and related needs.

❑ Focuses on developing understandings, skills, strategies, and processes to support or facilitate the learning of others.

❑ Seen as instrumental to leading.

❑ Aims at ensuring the capacity of the organization to operate as a learning organization.

❑ Delves deeply into the study of change processes.

❑ Seen as instrumental to lasting.

Expectations of Participants: Select no more than five of these.

❑ Deepen experience and enhance own expertise.

❑ Seek and use multiple perspectives to increase understanding.

❑ Monitor the results of their actions, practicing "successive approximation (taking a small step and monitoring its impact or result before taking another step)."

❑ Facilitate the learning or work of others.

❑ Ensure the sustainability of the organization in terms of desired changes and work.

❑ Focus on structure as they engage in problem identification, problem solving, and strategic planning activities.

(Continued)

Exhibit 5.1 (Continued)

Opportunities for Participants: Select no more than fourteen of these.

❑ Learn.

❑ Develop the dispositions of practice of professional learning communities.

❑ Ponder questions of mission and purposes for themselves as individuals.

❑ Find and understand the best tactics or ways of considering possible actions within the organization.

❑ Ponder questions of mission and purpose as they relate to the organization.

❑ Understand the big picture.

❑ Find and understand the best methods and strategies for their own actions.

❑ Identify and consider short- and long-term consequences of actions.

❑ Recognize unintended consequences where they emerge in their own actions.

❑ Surface and test assumptions that arise from their learning.

❑ Identify interdependencies in their work and in the work of those they lead.

❑ Look for and identify interdependencies in their work and in the work of the organization.

❑ Support the work of surviving changes in leadership, membership, governing policies, and so forth.

❑ Ponder questions of mission and purpose as they relate to leading.

❑ Explore complex cause-and-effect relationships.

❑ Identify interdependencies in the work of the organization.

❑ Explore the effect of mental models on people's perceptions of their current reality and the future.

❑ Find and understand optimum entry points and strategies for their work related to leading.

❑ Manage internal and external dissonance.

In one of the professional learning communities we recently created, the purpose of the community was "to develop a learning community that will deepen individual and organizational capacity to engage in sustainable school improvement in the service of learning." The organization that asked for this work determined that one of our roles as outside facilitators was to define the community's goal and even its purpose. In a different community we recently formed, this one housed in a school building, the school principal has determined that everyone in the building will eventually be part of a community that learns, leads, or lasts in service of adult and student learning, and that all staff and students will be invited to select the community they want to join. The process of defining the specific goals of these communities will involve the communities' participants.

PARTICIPATION AND MEMBERSHIP

Determining the size and composition of the community is another key factor in its creation. Communities can be small, with ten or fifteen members, or large, with seventy or eighty. They can include a subset of the people who work in an organization or may encompasses the entire organization. Ideally, those in a community should always want to be in it. They can include people who share roles and responsibilities, as is the case of a classroom community or a community of school principals. They can also include people who work inside an organization and have very different roles. They can even include outsiders such as community members since they too have a stake in the work of schools.

Some cross-role learning communities can experience problems related to positional leadership. These problems result from having people in a shared space who have more or less power within an organization, but who are not supposed to exercise their ascribed power in the context of their group work. Some teachers have difficulties negotiating their own identity when they are given roles and titles such as "lead teacher" or "master teacher," and others have difficulties speaking freely in front of people whose titles are "superintendent" or "university professor."

Under certain conditions, problems associated with positional leadership tend to disappear, and communities are able to proceed with the work of school improvement without being sidetracked by the politics of their role or organization. These conditions emerge when the professional learning community is so diverse that it encompasses multiple roles related to the world of schools, including superintendents, parents, teachers, administrators at different levels, coaches, professional developers, university faculty, social workers, guidance counselors, and students; when individuals with these roles come from different organizations; and when there are no majorities in terms of roles. Sometimes when the community members have different roles and titles inside the same organization but some of these conditions are absent, a facilitator needs to help them identify and negotiate their roles relative to positional leadership. In general, the less diverse the group is, the more work a community needs to engage in to depoliticize its discourse, create a safe climate for risk taking and innovation, and manage the potential development of cliques.

The community can have a shared purpose and a collective identity that transcends individual positions and politics with needed support and through processes that cultivate individual and collective expertise. As participants in such communities legitimize their individual voices and discover their collective voice, they can rise above the confines of their individual professional responsibilities and focus on effecting positive changes with their peers or within other organizational structures in their school or district.

LEARNING OPPORTUNITIES

The learning opportunities that the community provides for its participants depend largely on the community's purpose or reason for being. In a community that learns, the learning opportunities will focus on contributing to the expertise and experience of individuals. In a community that leads, learning experiences will focus on leading and facilitating. In a community that lasts, participants will learn how to understand and shape their organization to sustain learning for everyone.

Learning opportunities also vary depending on the membership of the community. In some communities, learning is targeted to selected individuals or roles, whereas in others, learning opportunities target the interests and needs of cross-role groups. The kinds of experiences a community provides for its members also vary with the developmental level of the community. In a beginning community, they tend to be provided at prescribed times and in a predetermined manner. In a developing community, learning opportunities may be provided at prescribed times, but follow-up and application activities may be partly determined with community members. In an established community, learning opportunities are provided as they are needed, determined by the community, with much of the learning occurring outside the meetings. In a systemic community, learning experiences arise from members' inquiry; scheduled time is used primarily for formal sharing of work, feedback, and discourse.

ALIGNMENT OF INDIVIDUAL AND ORGANIZATIONAL WORK AND NEEDS

Some of the work of developing professional learning communities entails securing the readiness and deepening the capacity of individuals in the organizations who may support them. The mediation of the relationship between the participants' individual work and needs and those of the organization they represent or support is ongoing and ultimately shapes the work of the learning communities. While it is critical that participants engage in research, inquiry, and writing activities on deeply valued issues or problems related to their professional thinking or their practice, it is equally important that their work makes a tangible contribution to the increased well-being or health of the participants' own sponsoring organization.

Once participants have joined the community, the facilitator and community members should explore their own organization and develop a shared vision for improving it. Questions that the community can explore in this context include:

- What do we want our organization to be like or have achieved ten years from now? Five years from now?

- What is my place in this system, and how do I relate to and function with others in and outside this organization?

- How does my perspective and that of others influence how I view and what I can do in this organization?

- What are my organization's qualities, needs, and problems?

- How can I best influence and support my organization?

As individuals explore their needs and those of their organization, they may ponder questions related to the identification and selection of a specific issue, topic, or problem for their work—for example:

- What are the things I know how to do well that benefit the organization I work for?

- Who benefits from my work?

- What can I learn more about and investigate that will increase my effectiveness and impact in terms of improving teaching, learning, and schools?

- What need in my organization is addressed by the work I want to do?

- How will my work have a positive influence on my colleagues, teachers, students, and other members of the educational community?

- How will it contribute to improvements in teaching and learning?

Professional learning communities need to engage in reasoned processes to identify the organization's needs and distinguish problem symptoms from real organizational needs. A department chair may assume that the problem in the school of education is that faculty members do not have adequate time for collaboration, and may want to pursue research and work around scheduling. But further analysis and a consideration of the different patterns and relationships that plague the school of education and the university system may yield a different understanding. The chair may discover that the problem instead is that the departments are offering far too many different types of courses and tracks and are exceeding their capacity to address goals related to quality and faculty development in the name of providing students with attractive offerings. A parallel situation might plague a high school where a principal is trying to mediate the need to promote interdisciplinary curriculum design with a district goal related to increasing the school's offerings of Advanced Placement courses, International Baccalaureate courses, and vocational tracks.

Defining and increasing the potential for community members to make significant contributions to the community and their organization is accomplished by helping participants identify a leadership role that is congruent with their sense of identity as professionals and with the community's purpose. Different people can handle or embrace different roles, regardless of their positional title. For one classroom teacher, an appropriate role may be that of mentor or coach to other teachers, whereas another teacher may be a good choice to chair a district task force. The same be true for principals and others.

An issue in maximizing the potential contributions of individuals to their organization lies in the nature of the alignment between individual interests and the needs of their own organization, or in the alignment between a school's interests and those of one or more organizations that sponsor professional learning in a school. Sometimes the problem is not one of assessing organizational needs appropriately, but of having these needs co-opted. In this context, the kinds of issues and questions that individuals are concerned or passionate about may not relate to a critical or important organizational need. This would be the case if an individual was passionate about the performing arts but the school defined itself as a science magnet.

Other examples of misalignment could occur if a school ignored or underemphasized the lack of congruence between its organizational priorities and its support for an outside provider who has different priorities. This would be the case if, for example, a school that had a commitment to literacy programs and practices and respected individual student differences hired an outside provider whose prescribed reading program was rigid and only partially addressed the literacy needs that the school had identified. Such misalignment would more than likely result in a staff who finds little relevance in learning together about a program or does not feel supported by its organization.

If a misalignment of needs and priorities separates the organization from its members, it will be important to address this gap so that both the individuals and the organization value the work to be done. Frequent and ongoing communication between the individual and different stakeholders in their organization is the most secure path to maximizing the alignment of individual and organizational needs.

RELATIONSHIP BETWEEN THE COMMUNITY'S WORK AND ITS SUPPORTING ORGANIZATION

In the best-case scenario, as would be the case of a community that operated at the systemic level, community members and outsiders will recognize the community as an entity whose learning results in innovations and provides a model for other organizations striving to improve teaching and learning. At the other end of the continuum, community members and outsiders view the community as a select group convened to address a specific problem or task. In developing communities, insiders and outsiders see the community as seeking to improve the practice or performance of community members, whereas in established communities, insiders and outsiders view the community as existing to develop and improve practices for the betterment of the organization.

DISPOSITIONS OF PRACTICE AND PROCESSES THAT SUPPORT THE COMMUNITY

The extent to which the dispositions of practice are nurtured and practiced in learning communities is also dependent on the community's level of development. Whereas systemic communities embed and weave the dispositions into the fabric of the community, evidencing them in participants' thinking, beliefs, behaviors, and work and using them to help the community make decisions about its learning, the dispositions in beginning communities are external to and separate from the routines and practices of the community. As communities evolve, they begin to frame activities that incorporate the use of the dispositions and incorporate them into community members' self- and peer assessment, reflection, and goal setting.

START-UP AND OPERATION PROCESSES

The launching and continued support of professional learning communities involves a number of different considerations. These include defining the roles and responsibilities of facilitators and participants, recruiting and inducting community participants, and logistical concerns related to scheduling and location of meetings, and using processes that develop the dispositions of practice.

Facilitator's Roles and Responsibilities

A new community needs a facilitator to provide the conditions and enact the processes that will support its work. The facilitator can be internal to the organization or from outside. Internal facilitators may need to deal with any issues or politics that result from their position or role in the organization. The roles and responsibilities associated with facilitation include recruiting and inducting participating members and assisting the organization and the community in the assessment and development of individual and organizational readiness for learning communities. They also involve supporting the use and internalization of the processes that the community and its members draw on in the articulation and pursuit of work.

To help the community explore its role in capacity building, the facilitator may engage its participants in learning experiences that answer questions such as the following:

- What is a professional learning community?
- What is capacity building?
- What is the relationship between capacity building and professional learning communities?
- What are the different types of learning communities?
- What kinds of learning communities exist in my organization?

The facilitator can also provide participants with opportunities to identify and explore their own experience and expertise through questions such as:

- What am I passionate about studying?
- How does my passion or topic connect to my vision for my organization and its needs?
- What are the nature and complexity of those needs?
- Who is my constituency?

At some point, and depending on the circumstances that led to the creation of the learning community and the role and position of the outside facilitator, it may be necessary for the outside facilitator to engage community members in an exploration of their own governance and internal facilitation needs. In other words, the role of facilitation can be shifted to the community itself, provided the community is versed in the processes that will help it grow.

Recruitment and Induction Issues

The first consideration in identifying the potential contributions of individuals to their organizations is to recruit individuals who have the skills, knowledge, and dispositions of practice of professional learning communities and want to make a difference in their organization. Some of the questions that may assist in identifying individuals who could participate in professional learning communities include:

- Who are the individuals in our organization who can best understand the values and purposes of our organization?
- Who has a strong belief in equity and democratic processes?
- Who can be strategic about matters that relate to school improvement?

- Who has a solid understanding of teaching and learning?

- Who has the ability to develop capacity in colleagues and in the organization?

- Who has a sense of moral purpose?

- Who wants to make a difference?

It is also important to determine who will decide who should be included in a community. In one of the professional learning communities we are currently supporting, the principal convened an interim leadership group comprising representatives from all school constituencies (teachers, students, counselors, support staff, parents, community members) whose tasks included involving all members of the school in selecting a learning community they wanted to join; ascertaining the needs and interests of all constituencies; and developing the induction processes for the different communities. One of the tools this group used for recruitment and induction was the self-assessment in Appendix C.

Students as Participants

As someone who has facilitated professional learning communities for over fifteen years, I often wondered if it was truly possible to do justice to discussions of teaching and learning without students in the community. In education, we tend to shy away from involving students as partners in our exploration of issues and problems that students face. We often develop policies, programs, and experiences that affect students directly and indirectly without soliciting their thoughts in the process.

Students possess tremendous experience and expertise in the areas of teaching and learning. Their experiences as learners in schools are far more grounded in the reality of schools than are those of most adults. Through their multiple interactions with teachers, administrators, and other adults, they have firsthand experiences that affect their learning, either positively or negatively. They live teaching and learning every day.

Students can explore and play the same five roles that other community members can play. They can engage in the exploration of their own and others' learning and reflect on their learning and their thinking. They can conduct inquiry and research, design experiences or processes to be used in their schools, and develop themselves as facilitators of students' or others' learning.

Students' role in the learning community cannot be emphasized enough. Their participation in the community's work provides a refreshing reminder to its members of the inherent value of giving a voice to those who stand to gain or lose the most by its efforts. They help ground the voices of those of us who are adult participants and increase our consciousness about how we can choose to use language to be understood, impress, create distance between us, or bring us closer. Their presence becomes a vivid reminder of the real urgency of our work and the importance of doing good things to others and for others. Appendix G offers a rubric for assessing students' capacity to participate in professional learning communities.

Time and Place

The community needs to meet enough times during the year to have a sense of continuity and to be able to engage in needed exploration, inquiry, and design of processes and products. Although I cannot assert a definite number of days or hours a community needs, our experience supporting professional learning communities is that they work best when they meet every four to seven weeks and have some sustained continuous time to work together at some point in the year. One of the professional learning communities we facilitate meets seven days during the school year in three clusters of two days each, plus one day in May. It also meets five days in the summer and sometimes another five days for a writing retreat. Other professional learning communities we support meet once a month during the school year and five days in the summer.

Regardless of the number of days, it is important that the organization that houses or supports the community secures both the time and a space that is conducive to learning and collaborative work. Having access to computers and other instructional technology is also welcomed since much of the work of community members is inquiry based.

Participants' Roles

The work of professional learning communities is influenced greatly by the assumptions and beliefs that their participants have of themselves and others. For many individuals who join professional learning communities, the primary goal is to be in a place and with a group of other learners with whom they can share questions, ideas to be tested, and projects in the making. In other words, the professional learning community is a place to belong.

One way of helping participants in professional learning communities situate themselves and their work within the community is to have them explore five different, though often interconnected, roles: learner, reflective practitioner, researcher, designer-author, and presenter-facilitator.

Participant as Learner   Whether pursuing new areas of interest and inquiry or continuing to explore and probe facets of learning in others, participants are active, avid learners who document and share their questions, discoveries, and knowledge in the professional learning community. They do so through the processes and products that the community supports.

Members of professional learning communities use the community to deepen their learning and stretch their thinking, as evidenced by this participant's comments:

> This community has made me challenge myself to improve as a
> learner and educator, and to critically examine my curriculum choices
> and assessments. It can be an unsettling process at times, but I know
> that when I am feeling most in a state of disequilibrium, I am about
> to experience tremendous growth and things are about to fall into
> place. This community continues to provide that catalyst.

Participant as Reflective Practitioner   Reflection is the cornerstone of the professional learning community. Active, open questioning and feedback on each other's practice are central to the development of all the dispositions of practice of professional learning communities. Each member sees himself or herself not only as a professional, rigorously investigating his or her own practice, but also as a colleague helping others document and refine their practice. This ongoing reflection is embedded in each community gathering through peer review sessions, conferences with facilitators, or final reflections at the end of each day. In Communities for Learning, reflection is also evident in much of the fellows' written work, including the portfolios they produce at the beginning and end of their fellowship experience, as this participant noted:

> On a day with this community, I know that I will be challenged to
> think deeper, work harder, listen more carefully, and respond more
> thoughtfully than I did the day before. It's difficult to put into

words—a bit of a paradox—but in this community, nothing I think I know is sacred, and everything I believe is valued.

Participant as Researcher   In the spirit of educational inquiry, many participants in the professional learning community pursue action research projects as the core of their work. These are research studies designed by individuals or teams around a compelling question that ultimately will inform practice. The data for this research are collected in the field—in the participant's own work setting or a setting that is of interest to the community. The following quote illustrates that the inquiry process is cyclical rather than linear, always leading to new insights as well as new questions.

At one point I asked myself, "When will my journey end and what will my destination, my final product look like?" And my response was, "You will never be done. You will always have more questions and, furthermore, perhaps it is not the final product that has exclusive value. Perhaps it is the very process of questioning that has most value.

Participant as Designer-Author   An integral aspect of each participant in the professional learning community is the articulation of his or her expertise and experience. This is often accomplished through the design and publication of work that may include curriculum or assessment units, courses and professional development protocols, action research studies, articles, or books. The process of designing a well-thought out curriculum unit produces much more than a series of connected lessons. It often helps teachers articulate previously unquestioned assumptions, consider the trade-offs among desired outcomes for students, reconcile issues of breadth and depth, and grapple with the best approaches for collecting data on student learning. The following quote underscores an appreciation of the value of curriculum writing processes.

I wanted a community of learners. I knew there was always something I had not asked, had not accomplished. . . . I knew it was process and not only product that mattered. And this community is about process; good product is the result of paying great attention to process.

This community is my quiet place. It has resurrected the writer in me. It is the springboard for intellectual pursuits and stimulating conversations.

Participant as Presenter-Facilitator Members in professional learning communities are committed to documenting and sharing their thinking. They do this in various ways, often through the direct facilitation of the learning of others and through the formal dissemination of their work in seminars or at conferences. The following quotation illustrates the fact that learning communities provide members with a risk-free environment to practice and hone the knowledge and skills they want others to learn about and use:

> I have come to pride myself on being able to design fairly tight and rigorous programs that transition smoothly from one section to the next, and require minimal "emergency intervention" on my part to salvage or move sections during a session. While being responsive to participants' needs is always part of the picture, it is very different from feeling as though you have to "save" your program, which is how my second session felt. Worse still was the feeling that I was unable to salvage it, like I was watching it fall and kept trying to grab it, but missed every time—nightmarish . . . frustrating . . . and humbling. . . .

> There were some very real factors that impacted the second session, which just didn't gel from the start. The individual activities themselves were, for the most part, solid—but the session as a whole just didn't feel quite right, in spite of the fact that I'd spent lots of time thinking it through and changing and manipulating activities.

Developing Dispositions of Practice

The processes that participants in professional development communities engage in support the development of the dispositions of practice. They include individual and collaborative inquiry, dialogue, data analysis, reflective writing, portfolio development, text-based discussions, peer reviews and feedback, mentoring, and design activities. The majority of these processes incorporate dialogue, as defined by Yankelovich (2001). They involve collaborative discourse in which all participants assume that no one knows or has a complete understanding of any one issue but that, together, the group can attain it. Supported by the disposition of Commitment to Understanding, they entail listening to understand and make sense of ideas.

Intellectual Perseverance, plus Courage and Initiative, are also exercised as participants engage in processes that entail revealing their assumptions in ways that allow them to be scrutinized, reexamining their positions and the positions of others, and searching for and valuing multiple perspectives, so they can practice, more than anything else, being comfortable with ambiguity and with questions that may be difficult, if not impossible, to answer.

These processes may not unfold in the same way in every professional learning community. For example, in a regional professional learning community of teachers, administrators, and professional developers from thirteen school districts, the participants negotiated the agenda of a week in the summer, three years into their work as a learning community. Table 5.1 shows the feedback of one of the community members to a summer agenda draft.

In another learning community, participants engage in a text-based discussion using a structured protocol developed by McDonald, Mohr, Dichter, and McDonald (2003) that supports the development of Commitment to Understanding and Intellectual Perseverance. In this protocol, participants engage with a specific text in a discussion and through reflective writing (see Exhibit 5.2). The discussion is driven by the connections that participants make to the text and by the use of specific guiding questions. The protocol requires that participants revisit the text to ground their inferences and conclusions, while at the same time allowing them freedom to generate their own personal interpretations.

The values and norms of the community support this collaborative discourse, creating a climate of equality and enabling participants to explore a common ground and listen with empathy. This is especially true when there is diversity of roles in the professional learning community. As Yankelovich (2001) stated, "The methods of science and professional expertise are excellent for generating factually based knowledge; the methods of dialogue are excellent for dealing with this knowledge wisely" (p. 191).

Table 5.1
Draft Agenda and Participant's Comments
for a Summer Institute

Day	Proposed Plan	Participant's Comments
Monday 8:30–3:30	Agenda review Introduction to unit design components and template Review of exemplary units Identification of organizing center Identification of essential and guiding questions Selection of standards and indicators to be assessed	Okay, although it seems like a packed agenda
Tuesday 8:30–5:00	Unit context and overview Preliminary rationale Development of diagnostic, formative, and summative assessments Work on data analysis from member schools (optional)	Still confused about the terms diagnostic, formative, and summative
Wednesday 8:30–3:30	Sketching of rubrics, checklists, and learning opportunities Sharing how participants have used their work in the schools	We may need more time for the sketching
Thursday 8:30–5:00	Peer review Selection or development of reflection prompts Process statement Portfolio organization Mini session on grading and reporting out (optional)	The peer review should happen first thing in the morning so we can use the feedback in our reflection
Friday 8:30–12:30	Bringing the work to the schools Shoebox sharing *Note:* Activity that involves collecting artifacts that represent one's learning and placing them in a closed shoebox. These artifacts are often shared as a culminating activity.	This is important—I don't know how to best share what I have learned here.

Exhibit 5.2
Rich Text Protocol for a Discussion

Purpose: Enables group to take apart a text element by element

Time: Up to an hour

Group size: 5–15 participants

Steps

1. Assign facilitator, recorder, and timer.

2. Facilitator describes the content of the text and previews the steps involved in reading. This includes the modeling of descriptive statements in step 3. (5 minutes)

   "I noticed that the author uses x definition of leadership."

   "The author develops an argument about education using three premises."

   "The last paragraph of the article describes a previously unstated assumption about capacity."

3. The group rereads the text using the following guiding question, jotting down ideas in the margins, underlining sections, and so forth: "In what ways can our attention to the leadership dimensions described help us allocate our human and other resources to schools, or refine or change our strategies for working with schools to increase their effectiveness?" (10 minutes)

4. In a go-around, each participant shares one to three elements she or he noticed. No interpretation is allowed. The recorder records everyone's observations on a chart. (10 minutes)

5. The facilitator asks the group if any observation needs "checking out" by revisiting the text. (2–3 minutes)

6. The facilitator guides the group in the selection of one to three items on the chart they generated in step four that would be fruitful in discussing further and encourages participants to generate interpretations of those items. No direct challenges to the interpretations are allowed. (10 minutes)

(Continued)

7. The facilitator asks participants to select one idea from the text under study and write about it based on a particular perspective or theory she or he has. (5 minutes)

8. Participants pair off and share their writing with each other, challenging each other as appropriate. (10 minutes)

9. One at a time, participants say one thing they learned about the whole text based on their experiences with the protocol. (5 minutes)

Source: McDonald, Mohr, Dichter, and McDonald (2003).

ASSESSMENT

Professional learning communities can use specific tools to support the community's learning processes and its work. Some of these tools center on the community, whereas others focus on the organization that houses the community. If the community and its supporting organization are the same, the tools used to assess the community are, in essence, also assessing the organization. If the community is a subset of the organization or is separate from it, the measures used to assess the community are only peripherally related, or even unrelated, to the organization.

Community-centered measures support the assessment of a community's focus as well as its overall development or maturity. Because some communities can be created to focus on learning, leading, or lasting, individuals who are charged with assisting in the creation of different learning communities can use these measures to guide their recruitment and selection processes. Once the communities are formed, their conveners, as well as their members, can also assess the community's growth over time. In addition, these measures have been constructed so that raters who score the community at a low level of readiness can look at the descriptors of higher levels to identify potential interventions that might increase the community's ratings. A community that learns could use the rubric in Appendix D to assess its evolution over time. A community that leads can use a similar rubric (see Appendix E). Table 5.2 contains an excerpt of such a measure, focused on the community's purpose. A community that lasts can use a different rubric (see Appendix F), as illustrated in Table 5.3, focused also on the community's purpose.

Table 5.2
Partial Rubric for Assessing Purpose for
a Community That Leads

Beginning Community	Developing Community	Established Community	Systemic Community
Focus on leading is to prepare selected individuals for specific leadership roles or events	Focus on leading is to develop an understanding of and improve leadership skills	Focus on leading is to promote best practices in leadership	Focus on leading is to support leadership that will promote learning for everyone
Learning is geared to certifying leaders	Learning is geared to developing leaders	Learning opportunities focus on developing leadership	Learning opportunities focus on deepening understanding and abilities related to best practices in leadership

Table 5.3
Partial Rubric for Assessing Purpose for
a Community That Lasts

Beginning Community	Developing Community	Established Community	Systemic Community
Purpose of learning is specific to the needs of organizing a group	Purpose of learning combines individual interest or passion with learning about how to maintain the community	Purpose of learning is connected to organizational development and funding	Purpose of learning is to develop and deepen areas of individual expertise as well as focus on questions and issues of sustainable change
Learning focuses on what it means to learn in a community and the relationship between and among individuals in the community	Learning focuses on the relationship between individuals and the organization	Learning and discourse are focused on questions of viability and sustainability	Learning processes and structures focus on supporting and promoting the sustainability of the community and its learning

A different measure assesses participants' perceptions on the extent to which a group operates as a community by asking participants to use a rating scale on items such as these:

- Shared understanding of the learning tasks and goals of the community
- Willingness among community members to reveal themselves so that all can learn through accessing each other's perspective
- Willingness among members to step in and perform needed roles and behaviors, regardless of their formal position.

This measure is included in Exhibit 5.3.

The measure can be administered periodically so its members can assess indicators of more or less growth for the community as a whole. Depending on such assessment, community members or facilitators may identify strategies to improve the community's ratings. For a cross-role learning community, the measure can be modified to identify the different roles of respondents to determine how participants who have different roles in the organization view the community as a whole.

Organizational measures focus on the readiness and capacity of the school, district, or other educational organization to house or support professional learning communities aimed at improving schools. One such measure is a survey that assesses organizational support for professional learning communities in three domains: support for the community's learning, the community's expectations, and the community's opportunities. A rating scale for assessing such organizational support is presented in Exhibit 5.4. *"For example, in offering opportunities for such communities, some organizations assign roles and responsibilities as a way of returning favors or promoting political agendas, whereas in other organizations roles and responsibilities are predicated on members' experience and expertise. Some organizations reward compliance, whereas others reward innovation and inquiry."*

Another measure is an organizational rubric with indicators that span the continuum from readiness to capacity (it was described in Chapter Four and is included in Appendix B). This rubric is used in two primary ways. First, it serves as a conversational device to engage the formal organizational leaders and others within a school or district in the exploration of the dispositions of practice and their manifestations at different levels of readiness. Second, it is a diagnostic device, assisting members of the professional learning community in

Exhibit 5.3
How Have We Grown as a Learning Community?

Assign a rating to each item below that you think describes the current status of our professional learning community. Use the following rating scale: 1 = absent from everyone to 5 = evident in all of us.

Rating	Requirements of an Effective Learning Community
	1. Public knowledge of who and what we are as individuals.
	2. Public knowledge of the organization we represent.
	3. Shared understanding of the learning tasks and goals of the community.
	4. Broad awareness of individual goals and needs.
	5. Awareness of skills, knowledge, and other resources available within the community.
	6. Willingness among community members to reveal themselves so that all can learn through access to each other.
	7. Concern among members for each other's growth and learning: members are curious, make suggestions, and so on.
	8. Appreciation of and ability to seek out and learn from our differences and diversity.
	9. Awareness of methods for resolving conflict and ability to use them.
	10. Active rather than passive learning, including questioning as we learn.
	11. A willingness among members to step in and perform needed roles and behaviors, regardless of formal position.
	12. Knowledge about how to deepen our understanding and learning as we pursue our passions and address needs.
	13. A built-in, ongoing, self-assessment and feedback system for both individuals and the community.
	14. Built-in, ongoing support for each member.
	15. Numerous and diverse connections among individuals, small groups, and the whole community.
	16. Willingness and ability among members to work in different arrangements and group sizes.
	17. Consideration and respect for each other's learning needs and styles.
	18. Shared understanding of a common vision for improving teaching and learning.

(*Continued*)

Exhibit 5.3   (Continued)

Check the following category that applies to you:

Student _____

Teacher _____

Building administrator _____

District office _____

Professional developer _____

Parent representative _____

University faculty _____

Other _____

---

identifying the readiness levels of a school or district and helping them identify appropriate actions or interventions for increasing its capacity.

The following sets of actions were identified by a professional developer in her assessment of a school she had been supporting for a few months. She assessed the school at an awareness level in terms of the disposition of Commitment to Understanding and proposed the following activities for an upcoming professional development program.

- Assist department chairs from the different departments in the development of action plans to implement specific strategies related to classroom discipline.

- Ask the department chairs representing the different departments to collect classroom data related to their action plans and participate in peer review of the data collected.

These actions may help the different departments recognize the value of data related to monitoring the impact of classroom management and discipline-related strategies. It may also lead to their being able to develop specific data collection processes.

Organizations, like individuals, are not always poised to support professional learning communities. Communities themselves sometimes lose their momentum

Exhibit 5.4
Assessment of Organizational Support for Professional Learning Communities

1. In Support of the Community's Learning

		1	2	3	4
A	Ignores the learning and work of individuals				Provides opportunities and expectations for individuals to share what they are learning and thinking
B	Adopts and mandates "teacher-proofed" scripted programs				Promotes exchanges between teachers and others that would lead to developing and sharing expertise
C	Schedules required meetings that conflict with informal gatherings and groups				Creates opportunities and reasons for informal leaders to exercise leadership
D	Demands actions, paperwork, or attendance on such short notice that it is impossible for individuals and groups to prepare thoughtfully				Dedicates structured time to support thoughtful collegial conversations and work
E	Publicly attributes blame or praise for student achievement on specific individuals or groups				Assumes that everyone shares the responsibility and is accountable for ensuring that all students succeed

(Continued)

Exhibit 5.4 (*Continued*)

	1	2	3	4
F	Isolates new members from the rest of the community			Creates mentoring and other collegial structures that pair experienced and new members in ways that support the induction process
G	Teachers work in isolation of each other			Teachers engage in all kinds of collaborative work

2. In Support of the Community's Expectations

	1	2	3	4
A	Looks to outside "experts" for expertise			Assumes that the community and its members have expertise
B	Acknowledges and supports only formally declared, traditional leadership roles and top-down decision making			Promotes site-based and participatory decision-making and problem-solving processes that deemphasize existing hierarchies
C	Standards are adjusted based on external influences and are applicable to only some members of the community			Upholds high standards for the community and all its members

	1	2	3	4
D	Creates structures and policies that discourage discourse around teaching and learning and promote a pervasive culture of blame			Promotes collaborative approaches for problem finding, problem solving, decision making, scenario planning, and the production of work
E	Accountability is a threat, with roles and responsibilities at stake			Creates experiences that help everyone in the organization clarify and negotiate roles and responsibilities in ways that foster shared accountability
F	Distributes itemized lists of do's and don'ts related to teaching and learning			Provides formal and informal opportunities for conversations around student work, as well as vertical and horizontal articulation of expectations and criteria

In Support of the Community's Opportunities

	1	2	3	4
A	Assigns roles and responsibilities as ways of returning favors or promoting personal or political agendas			Assigns roles and responsibilities predicated on a recognition and respect for the leadership that teachers and other community members already have by virtue of their experience and expertise

(Continued)

Facilitating, Assessing, and Sustaining Professional Learning Communities **103**

Exhibit 5.4 *(Continued)*

	1	2	3	4
B	Promotes and rewards compliance			Promotes and rewards innovation and reflective professional inquiry
C	Mission, vision, and purpose, if articulated, belong only to those in power			Creates and supports a climate that fosters a shared mission, vision, and purpose for student learning
D	Prevents the community from convening or dismisses its existence			Provides administrative support for the community and its members
E	Carefully and consistently monitors activities and conversations of members			Provides multiple and safe opportunities for members to share questions, thinking, and work

or their sense of purpose. The measures we use to assess their work and their impact are one of the many components required to foster their development. The ongoing use of these tools throughout the drafting, feedback, refinement, and dissemination processes, and the resulting dialogues we have with the communities we facilitate, can promote the design and distribution of thoughtfulness.

Role of Feedback

Feedback plays a critical role in developing the expertise of participants and shaping the culture of a professional learning community. In a sense, feedback is the greatest equalizer. By holding everyone accountable to provide, receive, and attend to feedback, the work becomes the focal point and the different roles and responsibilities the background.

In learning communities, feedback is exchanged informally, as individuals and groups exchange ideas and offer possibilities, and formally, through structured peer reviews such as the peer review process, which we have adapted from Allen, Blythe, and Powell (1999). This peer review process is one of the mechanisms that several of the professional learning communities I support use to develop and maintain their standards and rigor. In this peer review process, practiced five or six times per year, participants present an idea, a piece of their work, or a question they are interested in exploring or refining. Acting as "critical friends," members of the peer review group give warm and cool feedback, helping the presenter to make new connections and see additional possibilities. In this context, warm feedback refers to comments that validate and show applications or connections, whereas cool feedback includes questions, confusions, and wanderings. Unlike Allen, Blythe, and Powell's original protocol, presenters do not engage in a dialogue with their peers at any time during the process of presenting or getting feedback on their work (see Exhibit 5.5).

Other formal ways in which feedback is produced and exchanged include using formal critiques between participants in professional learning communities who serve as critical friends of other participants who present their work at regional, statewide, or national conferences. One of the responsibilities of the facilitator is to model the feedback process and provide community members with exemplars or examples of best work to anchor the quality and depth of responses that defines the standard for the community. The following letter is an illustration of such an exemplar. It was written by Phyllis Beinstein, a literacy coach who works in an elementary school in the Bronx in New York City, to Liz Locatelli, a teacher and staff developer in Rockland, New York:

> Thank you SO much for the workshop you presented last week. It was extremely worthwhile. The content generated thoughtful and relevant discussions about several "big ideas":
>
> What are some meaningful ways to scaffold reading comprehension instruction? What IS reading comprehension? Which strategies are crucial for a reader to apply when constructing meaning from a text? What are the significant factors in transferring reading skills so that students can become proficient at reading independently? How does looking at the learning style of our students help to inform our instruction?

Exhibit 5.5
Feedback Protocol: Peer Review Using Warm and Cool Feedback

Format

- Four to five people in a group (preferably with people who have not worked together), with equal time to each member.

- Round robin.

- The presenter can steer feedback in a given direction by posing a question or need. Once the presenters have finished, they may not speak again.

- During feedback, a group member who has nothing to say can pass.

- If someone agrees with another's point, he or she dittoes.

Procedure

- Begin with rounds of warm feedback until you've exhausted it.

Warm Feedback Examples

- No praise

- Focus on relevance, applicability, and possibilities

- Examples:

   "You can also address x with . . ."

   "This could also be combined with . . ."

   "This might allow your students to understand . . ."

   "If you included the x teacher, you could also . . ."

- Proceed with rounds of cool feedback until you've exhausted it.

Cool Feedback Examples

- No negative judgments

- Focus on questions and confusions

- Examples:

   "I don't understand . . ."

   "Why did you . . . ?"

   "Could x have a negative effect on . . . ?"

Exhibit 5.5 *(Continued)*

The person receiving feedback cannot discuss or respond to feedback but can take notes.

- When everyone in the group has received feedback, people can seek clarification or discuss the feedback received.

Source: Allen, Blythe, and Powell (1999).

Your personal style was upbeat, appropriately expert, reflective, and validating to the contributions of participants. You had a diverse audience, many of whom were more knowledgeable about assessment than you had expected. You were able to note this, adjust your plan so that you deemphasized unnecessary background material, which felt like an invitation to the audience to become part of the presentation and share their expertise. . . .

Now, for the hard part: suggestions for reflection. I'm wondering if perhaps the afternoon piece could have been condensed. I noticed some signs of fatigue once we got to the third and fourth sections of the student commentaries. You might consider extending the time we had to discuss the possibilities for transferring some of the wonderful ideas generated during the workshop to our own sites.

Revising Goals and Action Plans

One of the processes aimed at increasing the viability of the professional learning community involves increasing individual and collective strategic and self-regulatory capabilities through the identification and continuous monitoring of goals and action plans. Following is an example of a process used to assist a team to continue its work in the district after leaving a meeting of a regional professional learning community:

1. Revisit the strategic planner that you completed in May, related to the focus you established for this week.

2. Revise that plan, if necessary, based on your current thinking.

3. Use the planning sheet to establish more specific guidelines for this week's work (set benchmarks, identify team responsibilities, and set deadlines for individual tasks and team contributions, etc.), tentatively schedule conferences and identify mini-sessions back in the district in which you will participate.

4. Finally, articulate an image of success for your work this week and post it in the posting area of this room. There should be a posting for each individual's image of success for their own week's work, and another that represents the image of success for the team's work.

Following is an example of a team's action plan summary for a middle school:

- Creation of professional development map with essential questions and monthly activities to be presented at faculty meetings

- Use of shared files for the continued development and implementation of learning strategies

- Start dialogue with peers from each grade level on what constitutes quality work

- Create a matrix of strategies for grades 5–8 and distribute it to each grade level so that teachers have a toolbox of best practices to use with their students.

PERMANENCE FACTORS

Learning communities vary in terms of the degree to which they can last beyond their current work or members. In beginning communities, the end date of the community is predetermined, whereas in a developing community, the community's existence is certain in the present and is dependent on factors outside its control to determine its future. In established communities, the responsibility and control over the future of the community are shared by both its membership and outside factors, but its existence can be compromised if both are not in harmony. Systemic communities have established mechanisms for responding to internal or external changes in ways that allow the community to maintain its viability.

The ultimate evidence of the sustainability of a learning community lies in its ability to survive and preserve the processes that keep it alive and growing even with changes in membership or leadership. Despite the fact that the rigid quality of school programs and policies may stymie their efforts and minimize the impact of their actions, resilient learning communities are able to redefine their work and strategies to effect positive change. They do that by situating themselves in ways that enable them to find a new point of entry for their efforts and activities. This can be seen in the case of a professional learning community whose focus was initially curriculum development in literacy but repositioned its work on literacy around teacher induction and mentoring processes related to effective teaching practices as a result of new district policies around curriculum.

Enduring learning communities uphold learning about themselves and their work as an attitude as much as an activity. They share a sense of interdependence and mutual obligation toward the shared purpose of improving schools. The main indicator of their viability is their ability to preserve their shared purpose and the essence of its work despite changes in the membership of the community and in the organizations that surround it. In a sustainable learning community, the community is more resilient than any of its members, possessing the history, culture, and legacy that enable new and old members to carry its mission and work.

Community Outcomes

Improving Teaching, Learning, and Understanding

The work of learning communities can have a profound impact on participants' thinking and work. This impact is evident in participants' products and processes, and in their attitudes, discourse, and commitments. This chapter characterizes some of the tangible and intangible manifestations of this impact by examining the types of work that learning community participants engage in, the questions they ask, and the actions they take. It also describes the tools and processes that participants in learning communities can use to assess their work.

It is 7:00 A.M. The only sounds from the second floor of the school are made by adults in one of the classrooms. Ten teachers, the guidance counselor, and the dean of students sit on student chairs at the periphery of the classroom facing a teacher, who is also sitting as she shares her perspectives on readings about literacy-related problems that children of migrant workers face in schools.

Another teacher asks the group, "Are there groups of students who seem to share some of these problems? What do you do when you find out that a student does not appear to understand what he or she read?"

The conversation is lively but focused, as different individuals respond and ask questions or make observations related to the literacy needs of students in this school.

Someone reminds the group that it is 7:45 A.M. Everyone gets up and moves to different parts of the school to get ready for arriving students.

At 9:45 A.M., three of the teachers who participated in the morning exchange and two of their students, all of them members of a district-based professional learning community, leave the school and walk to the adjacent high school building. They go to a ninth-grade mathematics class where they sit in the back, observing the teacher and students work through some problems. At 10:15 A.M., they walk to a social studies class and continue their observations. Over the course of the next hour, they watch students and teachers in different classes and settings, and at 11:15 A.M., they gather in the library with a team of ninth-grade teachers and building administrators to discuss differences and similarities in terms of teacher expectations for student learning.

A week later, a similar set of visits will occur when the sixth-grade teachers, each accompanied by one of her students, visit the elementary school. These rounds of observations and conversations among small groups of teachers and students in three buildings will culminate in a series of after-school meetings with the middle-level staff and their students, as well as representatives from the other two buildings, to discuss curriculum and assessment articulation needs.

The individuals leading this initiative comprise a district team that has identified K–12 curriculum articulation as a priority in need of attention, based on a series of community and district forums held a year before the initiative was in full motion. The inclusion of students in the team was deemed indispensable given their knowledge, perspective, and stake in the problem at hand.

If one were not witnessing the interactions that take place in the first part of the scenario, it would be hard to tell that there is a presenting teacher leading the conversation. It would also be difficult to appreciate that another teacher is seeking to connect instructional resources to teachers' practices. It would be impossible to know that this gathering was voluntary and driven by participants' interests and willingness to engage in deep conversations around teaching and learning. And yet that is precisely the case.

Our lack of access to the rich textures and nuances in the exchanges and pursuits of community participants makes it difficult to appreciate the processes and outcomes of that work. One has to be in a specific community, sharing and living the interactions, the questions, the nonverbal exchanges revealing empathy, sympathy, curiosity, passion, and uncertainty, to fully appreciate the outcomes of professional learning communities. The challenge of this chapter is to make vivid those outcomes to readers.

The work of professional learning communities is most effective when it stems from participants' areas of expertise, interests, and the needs of the constituencies they represent. When community members are fully invested in harnessing their passion to address an organizational need, the resulting outcomes can be extraordinary. These outcomes are manifested in tangible actions, products, performances, and processes, but they are also evident in many more intangibles that are at least as significant.

A CLOSER EXAMINATION OF THE WORK

The work of a professional learning community can be centered on student learning, adult learning, or organizational learning; of course, any of these demand attention to the other two as well. Participants who focus on student learning delve deeper into curriculum, instruction, and assessment work related to students. They explore, design, or adapt protocols and processes for analyzing student work or are interested in exploring one or more facets related to learning needs or to the interface between teaching and learning. They are driven by questions such as these:

- What does "good" curriculum and assessment look like?
- How can we best teach and assess different kinds of learners?
- What does differentiation look like?
- Can we differentiate instruction in an equitable and fair way?

Not evident to an outsider is that in the scenario that began this chapter, the teacher who facilitated the conversation about some of the literacy problems of migrant workers' children is deeply concerned about two of the questions in this list. Her ongoing work in a professional learning community involves revising units of study with lessons and assignments that address the literacy needs of recent immigrants, which informs the conversation depicted in the scenario. At the same time, she is trying to engage other practitioners in her school in a comprehensive effort to increase sensitivity to the needs of learners with different backgrounds.

Participants who focus on adult learning support individuals or teams who want to deepen their understanding of the processes and conditions that facilitate adult learning and address questions such as:

- How can we help teachers develop and use diversified assessments?
- How can we enable teachers and administrators to use data to assess student needs and inform instruction?
- What does job-embedded staff development look like?
- How do we induct new teachers into the school community?

What one could not have known by reading the short scenario at the beginning of this chapter is that the teacher who asked several questions of the group having to do with instructional practices is the convener of this monthly seminar. Driven by the belief that teachers learn best when engaged in meaningful conversations with other teachers, her work in the professional learning community is focused exclusively on developing job-embedded approaches to professional development that maximize collegiality. The learning community is her research and development laboratory.

In a professional learning community, teams or individuals who focus on organizational learning explore problems and issues related to organizational change, knowledge creation and dissemination, and the development of individual and organizational capacity. They address questions such as:

- How do we develop the leadership capacity of teachers in our school?
- What are the best ways of distributing leadership?
- What would a district plan for using data look like?
- How do we create a professional learning community in our school?

Hidden in the scenario at the beginning of the chapter was the fact that two of the individuals who are leading the learning in the K–12 curriculum articulation initiative described are working in the domain of organizational learning. Their work in the community is driven by two questions: What does a coherent curriculum look like? and What are the practices that will increase K–12 curriculum coherence and articulation? Their work in the professional learning community involves a serious exploration of these questions with other community members, coupled with the implementation of a tangible set of processes, including the classroom visits and the postvisitation conversations. In their learning community work, they are seeking to develop tangible processes that will eventually be used at the elementary, middle, and high school levels to increase the coherence and articulation of curriculum in all grades.

The intangible outcomes resulting from this work include the range of understandings resulting from each of the classroom visits and their subsequent debriefing, as well as those stemming from each of the visits with staff from the different buildings. Such insights shed light on the essence of teaching and learning, teachers' practices, student engagement and learning, expectations and standards for student work, classroom interactions, teacher-student relations, curriculum and instructional approaches, and more.

MANIFESTATIONS OF THAT WORK

Professional learning community members may engage in a wide range of activities: developing a vision for the community and organization that supports it, identifying the nature of the influence that each community member has on other members of the organization, collecting data on organizational needs and priorities, and exploring their individual passions and interests. These activities may yield concrete products such as vision statements, action plans, or research studies.

The work that individuals and teams in professional learning community produce depends on whether they are looking at actions to take in their organizations or products they develop as a result of their research and learning.

Actions vary greatly depending on the formal roles of participants within their organizations. They include assessing the readiness of their organization for specific school improvement efforts and innovations, evaluating the merits and shortcomings of different strategies and processes, assessing the intended and unintended consequences of current and proposed programs, and ultimately effecting one or more actions to support the organization's goals and needs.

For teachers, actions may include designing, implementing, or evaluating a standards-based and learner-centered unit of study; designing a scope and sequence document with course outcomes to guide their work during the year, such as the one developed by Caledonia-Mumford Central District in upstate New York through the facilitation of Deb Bussewitz, a language arts coordinator and fellow of

Communities for Learning (see Table 6.1); designing and implementing a course of study; developing, field-testing, and evaluating assessments of student learning, studying the merits and shortcomings of different texts or instructional approaches; facilitating the collaborative analysis of student work; working with peers around curriculum and assessment articulation; or engaging in research on their practices, student learning, on the interface between the two. These actions may result in tangible products such as curriculum units, course designs, and action research studies.

For professional developers, actions may include assessing the learning needs of various individuals or groups; and designing, facilitating, or evaluating professional development activities that meet the needs of different constituencies, including awareness, skill building, design, and leadership programs. They may also include conducting research on the effectiveness of specific approaches or on the impact of programs; coaching future facilitators; experimenting with various job-embedded professional development approaches; facilitating study groups; using walkthroughs as a professional development strategy; and coaching administrators in the staff evaluation process. These actions may result in professional development programs, protocols for working on schools, or completed research studies. For example, as a result of her research and experiences working in middle schools, Jo Slovak, a former professional developer and currently an assistant superintendent of a district in upstate New York, developed a professional development prototype designed for middle school teams of teachers and administrators. The activities in her three-day program help educators explore the philosophy of and research concerning middle schools and guide them in forming a vision for their school.

The work of university faculty may be similar to that of teachers and professional developers in that it could revolve around the creation of units, courses of study, or programs aimed at faculty members. It may also include assessment of current policies and programs related to the preparation and certification of teachers, administrators, and other professional who work in schools, as well as the development of partnerships between schools, professional development groups, and universities.

Actions for administrators may include developing communication systems for different individuals or groups within the organization; facilitating the access and use of data to support teaching and learning; designing protocols for solving specific types of problems in schools or districts; crafting an organizational mission and vision with staff members; developing structures that promote shared leadership in the school or organization; brokering the expertise of different staff members and

Table 6.1

Course Outcomes for Writing, Grade 2, Caledonia-Mumford Central School District

Creative and Expressive	Expository	Persuasive	Literary Analysis
Within this genre student will be able to:	Within this genre student will be able to:	Within this genre student will be able to:	Within this genre student will be able to:
(T) Develop an original piece based on personal ideas, experiences, and literature in a creative or expressive form suited to the topic, audience, and/or purpose.	(T/R) Establish topic, audience, and purpose to inform about a personal or classroom experience or a topic of interest.	(I/T) Write a paragraph to express an opinion or position taken on an issue.	(R) Write a sentence or more of their prediction relating to a text.
(R) Create a piece where writing and drawing are on the same topic.	(I) Establish topic, audience, and purpose in response to a variety of print and nonprint resources and/or personal experiences.	(T) Include details, facts, and/or examples to convince the reader of the position.	(T) Write a sentence or more making a text-to-text, text-to-world, or text-to-self connection.
(T) Write about ideas and/or personal experiences in sentences that have a logical sequence.	(T) Use an introductory sentence that states a main idea, supporting details/facts, and a sentence to summarize the nonfiction topic.		Compare and contrast two sources.
(T/R) Write a complete sentence to express an idea or a personal experience.	(I) Develop an organizing structure matched to the topic and purpose (e.g., compare/contrast, cause/effect).		Write a response after reading two or more types of text.
(I/T) Write one or more paragraphs about a topic and/or a personal experience.			Compare or contrast a variety of texts or text features in writing.
			Write a question or questions to help understand the story better.
			(T) Write an inference based on story information.
			Use specific evidence from the text to identify theme when writing.
			Write a response after reading a text.
			(I) Write a summary.
Required writing tasks:	Required writing tasks:	Required writing task:	Required writing tasks:
• Journal entry • Personal narrative • Poetry • Create an acrostic poem	• Graph, poster, or chart • How-to directions • Compare-and-contrast informational essay	• Persuasive paragraph/letter	• Personal response to literary text • Description/analysis of literary text with text-based details • Summary

Note: I means to introduce, T means to teach and evaluate, and R means to reinforce.

enabling them to learn from each other; mediating the needs of students and staff with different administrators and agencies; and identifying and finding ways of disseminating best practices to others in the school or organization. Their products include policies, programs, and research studies. One example of such products was developed by Lisa Boerum, the assistant superintendent of Little Flower District in Long Island, New York. Lisa designed a teacher evaluation process in which teachers generate questions for individual inquiry related to their practice, develop and annotate classroom lessons and assessments related to those questions, and analyze student learning before generating new goals and questions for further inquiry.

For students who are participants in a professional learning community, appropriate actions may include gathering data and conducting research on the needs and perspectives of other students and other stakeholders in schools; identifying and articulating their learning needs to other members of the professional learning community and partnering with teachers, administrators, or others in the exploration of those needs and the design of lessons and units that address them; organizing students in their schools and identifying relevant actions to develop for such organizational structures; and identifying, designing, implementing, and evaluating activities or programs to solve school problems or address school-related needs. Given the fact that students and student learning are the ultimate targets of the work of a professional learning community and that in most schools, the role of students in influencing what happens to them in schools is rather limited, it is important that students' role in the professional learning community be meaningful (Fletcher, 2005).

In the case of professional learning communities whose membership includes representatives of community groups, nongovernmental organizations, or state agencies, relevant actions may include brokering relationships or forging alliances between entities that support schools but have not collaborated before; facilitating discussions between administrators and teachers or parents; identifying and enacting policies and programs that address specific school needs; and evaluating the impact of existing policies and programs.

TOOLS THAT ASSIST IN THE DEVELOPMENT OF THE WORK

The work of community members benefits greatly from the use of models, explicit criteria, and design tools that are both product and process centered.

Product-centered tools support the work that participants create related to student learning, adult learning, and organizational learning. Participants who develop curriculum materials directed at students use curriculum and assessment criteria with supporting rubrics. Practitioners and administrators who develop programs and learning opportunities for adult learners use professional development program criteria with supporting rubrics. Those who carry out individual or collaborative action research studies do so using action research criteria and supporting rubrics and checklists.

Process-related tools, which may be articulated in the form of rubrics, checklists, and exemplars, support the means through which the work of professional learning communities and their participants is delivered or implemented. They also promote the development of the dispositions of practice.

Tools That Support Curriculum and Assessment Work

Some of the most significant products of professional learning communities directly affect teaching and learning. They include curriculum units, lessons, and assignments, as well as formal student assessment measures. The evaluation tools that support individuals in their development and use of these products can include templates for design, criteria and rubrics to develop and score specific components, and even exemplars and illustrations of different rubric levels. Exhibit 6.1 provides a list of criteria we have used to help members of professional learning communities whose work focuses on the design of units, lessons and assessments.

Using tools such as rubrics and checklists increases teachers' ability to apply criteria to their design and develop Intellectual Perseverance along with a Commitment to Expertise. Table 6.2 contains an excerpt from a rubric for a curriculum rationale.

In a professional learning community, a teacher might use this rubric in the context of developing an explicit justification for the time and effort required in designing, implementing, and revising a curriculum unit. Although such a rationale is not typically demanded of many teachers in schools today, learning communities create the space and structure for teachers to explore the question, "Why am I teaching this?"

The following rationale, written by Richard Hinrichs, a teacher from Mattituck-Cutchogue School District in Long Island, New York, would receive the highest score on this rubric. Following is an excerpt of his rationale:

> Is war ever justified? is a question that is, in fact, unanswerable. War
> causes inhumane suffering, barbaric responses, and intolerable grief.

Exhibit 6.1
Curriculum and Assessment Criteria

- Standards-related student learning gaps have been identified to guide the design of the unit, assessment, or lessons.

- References to state or national standards are explicit, distinguishing performance indicators and standards that are addressed from those that are assessed.

- Additional outcomes and standards have been articulated.

- There is an organizing center for the unit, assessment, or lessons that revolves around a concept, issue, problem, or essential question.

- The unit, assessment, or lessons include a rationale or statement describing its importance.

- The rationale answers questions such as: Why is this important or worth teaching and learning? How do you justify the time it will take to teach it? How will it improve the lives or thinking of students? How will it make them better or more informed human beings?

- The unit, assessment, or lessons include a brief context statement or overview that provides an introduction to and synopsis of the unit, assessment, or lessons.

- The unit, assessment, or lessons are supported by essential and guiding questions.

- The unit or lessons include a culminating authentic assessment.

- The unit or lessons include diagnostic and formative assessments that diagnose and monitor students' progress and provide opportunities for intervention.

- There are reflective prompts or questions that support students' thinking about their learning, the process, or the creation of a product.

- Explicit criteria, articulated in the form of rubrics or checklists, support key processes or learning.

- There is a sketch or unit calendar that lays out the structure and sequence of the unit, assessment, or lessons. It shows the relationship between and among the components of the unit, the relationship between the assessment and the lessons that precede it, or the connection between and among a series of lessons.

- Learning opportunities are clearly described.

- The unit, assessment, or lessons include a description of the reading, writing, or thinking strategies linked to the learning opportunities and assessments.

- A teacher commentary or reflection that addresses the process of creating the units or lessons includes a self-assessment of strengths and needs, identifies learning, and poses new questions that have emerged as a result of the design process.

- There is a list of necessary student resources.

- There is a list of recommended resources for teachers.

Under what circumstances should one fight? Is it better to live free of war but with restraints on one's freedom? The lasting image that will linger for students after completing this unit is that conflict rarely involves good vs. evil or right vs. wrong. When nations declare war, there are often underlying reasons with multiple causes. Students should understand that explanations should not always be taken at face value; that reasons are complex, not simple; and that conflicting points of view need to be carefully analyzed. People who disagree can learn from one another when positive attitudes dictate respect and all sides listen to reason. Only then can one arrive at their truth confidently.

The objective of this unit is for students to question motives and decisions involving armed conflict between nations. The essential question addresses the paradox of whether war is ever justified. I decided to have students study causes of five recent wars (WWI,

Table 6.2

Excerpt from a Rubric for Curriculum Rationales

1	2	3	4
Unclear and undeveloped	Clear but not fully developed	Clear and relevant	Eloquent and substantive
Leaves unit seeming trivial—"Why bother?" remains a question	Significance of unit is questionable	The unit seems important enough to warrant the time it will take	Significance of this unit is indisputable
Content knowledge, skills, and/or dispositions are unclear or disconnected from any discernable focus	Identifies the content knowledge, skills, and dispositions addressed	Clearly and specifically explains the value of the content knowledge, skills, and dispositions addressed	Clearly connects the value of the content knowledge, skills, and dispositions addressed to helping students prepare for the world outside school
Standards are misrepresented or omitted	Mentions that the unit targets standards	Explains why specific standards are targeted	Describes how the standards addressed and assessed are key to the importance of the unit

WWII, Vietnam, the Gulf War, and the War on Terrorism). . . . Students learn that it is acceptable to question and investigate policy, as well as to protest and disagree. It's possible for a few to sway public opinion and change the way things are. Here lies the importance of an informed and educated populace. Each issue encourages students to struggle with questions: Which side was right? Which side would I have been on? Was this war justified?

It is important for teachers to articulate a formal justification for what they do; moreover, the insights that they gain from pondering questions that result in the development of a rationale can be far reaching and even more significant than the tangible written rationales that introduce teachers' units or courses. Such questions include: Why is that unit worth teaching? What will students know, be able to do, and value as a result of studying it? What justifies the time and resources required to implement it? How will it make students better human beings?

In addition to rubrics, curriculum checklists that highlight attributes of quality lessons and assessments such as the use of critical thinking skills can also be used by community members to develop and refine their work in the classroom. Lessons that are informed by such criteria:

- Require thinking beyond the literal level of comprehension and tap the levels of analysis, synthesis, and evaluation

- Promote depth of understanding

- Require that students use their knowledge to form opinions, make decisions, or create authentic products or performances

- Enable students to ponder and ask different kinds of questions as the primary means of inquiry and engagement

- Demand that students reconcile the thinking of experts and their expertise by reading two or more texts that represent different aspects of a topic or different viewpoints (in primary grades, such access occurs through interviews and field experiences)

- Allow students to engage in a comprehensive thinking, design, or writing process and carry a piece through the various stages in search of the clearest or most powerful message

In a learning community, teachers or students may use these criteria to foster their Commitment to Understanding as they assess, refine, and rethink their experiences and practices or devise ways of creating or improving new ones.

Tools That Support Professional Development Work

Tools that support professional development work include design criteria, scoring devices, exemplars, protocols, and designs for professional development offerings in schools or districts. Table 6.3 includes a description and excerpt of the scoring criteria and rubric we have used to help professional developers understand the importance of creating flexible and responsive programs. Flexibility has to do with the extent to which the program allows participants to negotiate their learning and assessment tasks and enables them to make reasonable choices independently.

Table 6.3
Scoring Criteria and Rubric for Assessing Flexibility
in Program Design

1	2	3	4
Participants work with the same material using the same strategies and developing the same product	Participants have limited choice of content (they must choose from a list of topics); strategies or product are the same for everyone	Participants have a wide variety of staff-developer-generated choices of content or strategies	Allows teacher-generated choice of content and strategies
Time and deadlines are fixed	Participants may use different content or strategies but time is fixed with regard to the deadline for the product	Time allotment is flexible for different partici-pants but is not tied to the actual assessment demands	Time allotment is flexible for different partici-pants and to accommodate differences among the products or performances selected

Other tools that support the design of professional development work include design templates, such as the one in Table 6.4, used for community members to examine and consider alternative ways for facilitating adult learning experiences. Tools such as this can be used to mediate conversations among community member participants about what works and what does not. They can also be used as a scaffolding structure to design or revise new work and to promote Intellectual Perseverance, Commitment to Expertise, and Collegiality.

Tools That Support Action Research

Individual and collaborative action research studies can be directed at student learning, adult learning, or organizational learning. As with other work, they are guided by design criteria, scoring devices, and exemplars that guide design and refinement activities. Table 6.5 shows excerpts of a rubric used to monitor and assess the design of action research studies.

Table 6.4
Template for Selecting a Facilitation Strategy

Strategy	Description	Example	When Would This Be a Good Strategy to Use?
Directive teaching	Teacher presents information	Overview of portfolios and how teachers can use them	
Generative teaching	Facilitator invites creative imagery using metaphors and posing hypothetical or para-doxical situations	Draw a picture of good thinking	
Collaborative teaching and earning	Facilitator groups students in groups that maximize interdependence and distributed leadership	Carousel questions	
Inquiry-based teaching	Learners participate in their own construction of knowledge through questioning or research activities.	Use of critical challenges	
Design	Learners transfer knowledge and skills learned by designing something they can use	Lesson design	

Note: Carousel refers to the use of sheets of chart papers that include different prompts or questions to which participants respond at different times. Group members start with a specific sheet, respond to a question, and move to another sheet. This allows all members to gravitate to questions they feel more comfortable with as well as build on others' responses.

While it would be difficult to deny the intrinsic value of rubrics, checklists, and other devices such as templates used to articulate explicit quality criteria, such tools come alive when they support and mediate dialogue and feedback processes that result in powerful yet often intangible learning for participants in professional learning communities.

Table 6.5
Excerpts of a Rubric for Design of Action Research Studies

	1	2	3	4
Action taken	The design includes a vague and unclear mention of the action(s) taken	The design includes a general description of the action(s) taken that raises questions about why it/they were chosen	The design includes a clear and specific description of the action(s) taken with explanation of why it/they made sense and how it/they changed over time	The design includes a clear and specific description of the actions taken with an explanation of why they made sense and how they changed over time References to the researcher's past experiences and/or the work of other researchers further supports the choice of actions
Research question	Research question(s) are related to the general focus but are unconnected to the actions and/or too broad to guide research	Research question(s) are related to the focus but not explicitly connected to the actions or rationale Questions need to be refined to provide better guidance for data collection and analysis	Research question(s) are specific, researchable, and interesting questions that are linked to the actions and rationale Questions provide guidance for data collection and analysis	Prioritized research question(s) are researchable, specific, concise, interesting, and explicitly linked to the actions and rationale Questions provide the structure for data collection and analysis
Data collection	Lacks mention of specific techniques for gathering data	A single data collection technique is mentioned without information about how or when the data were collected	Clearly describes a specific data collection plan that reveals that multiple sources of data were collected to capture actions taken and the results of those actions	Clearly describes a specific and manageable data collection plan that includes multiple sources of data, the actions taken, and the results of those actions, and includes measures to document the researcher's thinking through the process

Processes That Support the Use of Tools

What enables the community members and the community at large to improve what it knows and does is the dynamic and interactive use of the kinds of measures I have described. When communities use these measures to support the assessment and revision processes, everyone benefits. Following is an original rationale written by a teacher from Region 1 schools in the Bronx who is developing an interdisciplinary middle-level unit centered on technology:

> According to the standards, students need to demonstrate understanding of the impact of technology. A good way to do this is to study transportation and its effects on the environment. This unit builds the foundation for understanding how transportation technology affects the environment. Students will learn about fossil fuels and their impact on the environment.

Table 6.6 shows the feedback she received from Joanne Picone-Zocchia, the community's facilitator, from a written review of her draft, using the rubric for rationales to structure the feedback. The feedback promoted her Intellectual Perseverance, and Courage and Initiative enabled her to produce a revised rationale. Following is an excerpt:

> Is technology our friend or our foe? Every day, there are new "advances" in technology, but are they truly moving us forward? This is a question that the youth of today will be forced to grapple with throughout their adult lives.
>
> Transportation is an area strongly impacted by technological advances. Fewer than 200 years ago, "pump prices" or gasoline were irrelevant and "horsepower" had a much more literal importance in moving goods and people from one place to another. Movement was difficult and often slow, requiring planning and attention to details of weather and beast. Today, we travel quickly and comfortably in airplanes, by train, bus or car. Can there be any question about the benefit of technology?
>
> Examining issues related to transportation allows students to begin to appreciate the complex and often multi-faceted relationship between technology and progress. These lessons build the foundation for this understanding. Students will learn about fossil fuels and their impact on

Table 6.6
Feedback on the Rationale for Development of a
Unit on Technology

Rubric	Feedback on Rationale
Justifies significance and relevance of lessons/unit to both students and teachers (answers the question, "Why bother?")	It is difficult to get a complete enough sense of the unit to be able to begin to address the question, "Why bother?" Though it sounds that understanding how transportation technology affects the environment would be a good idea, it is left to the reader to imply just how specific and significant the related learning might be.
Describes how addressing the content knowledge, skills, and dispositions included in the unit or lessons helps to prepare students for life outside school	The writing alludes to the importance of students' understanding the impact that transportation technology has on the environment, but fails to show how it develops content knowledge, skills, and/or dispositions in students that will prepare them for life beyond school. What is written is clear, but it lacks the detail necessary to justify the lesson's merit or importance.
Is supported by current research on best teaching and assessment practices (e.g., standards based, student centered, attends to diversity of learners through differentiated instruction)	There is no mention of the teaching or assessment practices inherent in the lessons, so it is impossible to ascertain the degree to which they align with current research around best practices. There is no mention made of the teaching or assessment practices that are part of this lesson.

the environment, recognizing both benefits and issues of their use. . . . Research and debate will round out their experiences as they delve deeply into an issue or question that they deem important. Is technology our friend or our foe? Every day, there are new "advances" in technology, but are they truly moving us forward? This is a question that the youth of today will be forced to confront throughout their adult lives.

Having access to structured opportunities to receive and provide feedback is critical to the development of quality work related to professional development work as well and to the development of several dispositions of practice, including Collegiality, Intellectual Perseverance, and Courage and Initiative. Following is the first draft of a team's professional development action plan:

> We will create a common language and tie student learning together from year to year. Students' use of literacy strategies will increase if we show them the connection and relevance of strategic learning and we will be able to move students to a plateau of higher thinking and learning.
>
> We want teachers to commit to a limited set of strategies and use them well. They also need a chance to share what works. We will ask them to identify and select best practices.

After a peer review session and feedback focused on the general nature of the original plan, the team produced the following revision:

> Teaching and learning are too often a "Learn Then Toss" process. We hope to build life-long learners by making thinkers of our students. To do this, we are focusing on learning strategies. Specifically, we want to develop in our peers and colleagues a shared commitment to "best practices" strategies that can be embedded into the curriculum so that students can become better thinkers and writers.

Implementation steps

1. 2005–2006: Continue with strategy discussion through at least three grade-level meetings and one faculty meeting. We will ask teachers to select a strategy and test it for at least three weeks by embedding it in lessons and assignments.

2. Gather and annotate artifacts to help teachers get a "better grip" on strategies (student work, exemplars, portfolio, etc.).

3. Summer 2006: Determine specific steps to implement plan with middle school faculty.

4. 2006–2007: Carry out plan with at least two teachers per grade level.

Role of Exemplars

Having access to exemplary products and processes is sometimes as important as it is to have feedback on one's work and is critical in the development of Commitment to Expertise. Following is an annotated exemplar of the revision process needed to shift a research question from a responsive level (where the research is primarily exploratory and no actions are necessary) to a proactive level (where the research requires the implementation of specific actions). This annotation, which appears in brackets, was developed by Diane Cunningham, a facilitator of several professional learning communities, including Communities for Learning, to assist a learning community in engaging in more proactive research work and to model Commitment to Reflection.

As a staff developer I wanted to improve the quality of the collegial circles that I was facilitating. My responsive action research question (exploratory) was, "How can I improve the collegial circle process to better support teacher learning?" [From the exploration, the researcher is able to identify *new actions* and hunches or reasons why they may be worth taking. Notice that the question does not reveal that the researcher is taking any new action. It is a general investigation question.]

I read several books and articles and analyzed data that I collected to see what problems were evident in my current circles. From my reading and analysis, I identified specific actions that the research suggested that would help with the problems I was having. [Here we see the exploration. Through reading and looking at what is currently happening, the researcher is getting ready to take action.]

Possible actions

1. *Embed ongoing group processing questions* so that problems and concerns are addressed collaboratively—this can increase a group's ownership over the process and build individual reflective practice.

2. *Use criteria for success* at the start, in the middle, and as the basis for evaluation—this would provide a common goal for the

group that should help them to stay focused and it could provide guidance in planning and assessing the value of the group's selected activities.

3. *Establish group norms* that are regularly reviewed and addressed—this should help groups to run more smoothly and would help to avoid the social struggles—it could hold members accountable to each other, rather than to me. [From the exploration, the researcher is able to identify *new actions* and hunches or reasons why they may be worth taking.]

SOME OUTCOMES ARE HARD TO MEASURE

Many other outcomes result from the work of learning communities that are far more elusive and less concrete than curriculum units, research studies, or professional development programs. In pondering how to articulate these, I am often left with questions like the following ones: How does one describe or measure increased efficacy, engagement, or sense of purpose? How does one document the increased understanding of one's own practice and of the people whom such practice affects? How do we catalogue someone's increased commitment to self-improvement or to making other lives better? And finally, how can we begin to document increased loyalty and empathy?

The products and processes generated by the professional learning community can make a significant contribution to the documentation of the wisdom of practice. They can enrich the space that is now occupied by the vast amount of literature on teaching and learning that has excluded the voice of practice in significant ways. When these products are generated in diverse communities where each member's experience can be enriched by other members' perspectives, they can break new ground in our understanding of schools as complex systems and of what it really means to inhabit them.

We have a long way to go in helping practitioners, students, and others who have not traditionally been part of the academic discourse on education find their voice and their genres in the products and processes they create. Professional learning communities, especially those that are diverse in composition and membership, can promote a much-needed exploration.

Evaluating the Growth and Expertise of Community Members

Participants in professional learning communities evolve over time. Their focus and attention, their concerns, their actions, and the work they produce changes as they and their community mature. This chapter is designed to provide readers with tools and measures for helping individuals who want to become a part of a learning community and those already in them to self-assess and monitor their thinking, development, and work over time. Participants in professional learning communities can create and use different evaluation processes and measures depending on the actions, products, and targets evaluated. These processes and measures are laden with the values the community upholds, so in a sense, they are biased. Some of these processes and measures are applied to products, and others are applied to the processes. The evaluation and monitoring devices that community members use to assess the quality, effectiveness, or impact of its work are the primary ways in which the community makes a contribution to its member organizations. By upholding transparent

Many of the tools included in this chapter were developed by Joanne Picone-Zocchia.

and rigorous standards and embodying them in tools and measures that others can use, the professional learning community promotes more thoughtful and rigorous routines and practices.

There are a number of measures for evaluating the individuals who inhabit learning communities. Individuals can use them to assess their readiness for, investment in, and work in professional learning communities. Because individuals exist inside communities and organizations, it is important to keep in mind when selecting a measure the specific purpose of a measure and the context in which it will be used.

Many of the measures discussed in this chapter raise respondents' awareness of criteria and values that they may not have otherwise thought about. In this way, they become interventions as well as evaluation tools. The tools in this chapter differ from measures included in the rest of the book by focusing primarily on the interests, commitment, involvement, contributions, and growth of participants in learning communities.

MEASURES OF INTEREST AND COMMITMENT

These measures can be used to recruit members into a specific learning community or to help them self-assess their degree of investment and involvement. The measure described in Exhibit 5.1 can help individuals who may be interested in joining a professional learning community select a community with their desired focus. This measure includes a number of items clustered around several areas, one of which relates to the relationship between the focus of the work an individual wants to pursue and his or her organization's needs or goals. Following are some of the items that an individual would choose from:

- I am not sure that my school needs anything from me beyond successful compliance with the rules and requirements that are put forth.

- Much of what I am interested in learning relates to existing initiatives or projects that come from needs in our school. Other interests are more connected to learning I am doing in other places or to what I see as the needs of students.

- I am drawn to questions and learning that connect to needs I see in our teachers and students.

- The ideas, learning, and questions that I care about are all directly or indirectly related to the needs that I see in my school.

To help potential participants in professional learning communities decide on whether they have any interest in belonging to a professional learning community, they can use the measure in Table 7.1 and determine their level of investment in different community areas. This measure can assist conveners of learning communities in framing recommendations regarding the actual number of communities that can be formed inside an organization, as well as in the assignment of specific individuals to these communities.

MEASURES OF GROWTH AND ATTAINMENT OF DISPOSITIONS

In addition to assessing their specific interest in particular learning communities, individuals can assess themselves and their organization in terms of the extent to which they embody the dispositions of practice. One such measure involves having them color or shade the extent to which they and their organization possess these dispositions. Figure 7.1 illustrates this kind of a measure.

A more sophisticated measure consists of the individual rubric to help participants assess their dispositions of practice along a readiness-capacity continuum. This rubric is found in Appendix A. Community members may use it as a self-assessment by highlighting their current practices and identifying goals for their work in their organization and in the community. An adaptation of this measure, directed at students, is included in Appendix G. Table 7.2 portrays the equivalent dimension related to using work that is found in the adult measure.

We have used both the student and adult measures as a baseline measure and a formative device. As a baseline measure, we have asked individuals to self-assess once they join a learning community. As a formative device, we have used it to help participants monitor themselves and their growth in terms of the dispositions of practice.

In addition to readiness assessments, some learning communities decide to use a formal application and induction process. In such communities, members use one or more of the preceding measures to produce a baseline portfolio as a part of their formal induction into the community. At Communities for Learning, this process includes the development of a baseline portfolio that begins with a formal application letter and is completed during the first six months of

Table 7.1

Self-Assessment of Degree of Involvement in Professional Learning Community

	Beginning	Developing	Established	Comprehensive
Perspective (my reasons for being involved)	I am involved in this learning community primarily to increase my own learning and capacity	I am involved in this learning community to increase my own learning so others like me benefit	I am involved in this learning community to use my learning to make a positive change for others in my organization	I am involved in this learning community to use my learning to affect education in important and lasting ways
Dispositions (the role of the dispositions in my thinking and work)	I understand that the dispositions are present in my thinking and work, but I have yet to recognize them	I have self-assessed for the presence of the dispositions, and I now know where my strengths and needs lie	I have purposefully developed the dispositions in my thinking and work	I have internalized the dispositions and shared them with others
Work with others (whom I prefer to work with)	I prefer to work and think primarily as an individual	I gravitate toward like-role groups to support my thinking and work	I seek groups with multiple roles represented to push my thinking and work	I solicit cross-role groups to review and give feedback on my thinking and work
Learning (my learning needs)	I am focused primarily on my own needs, interests, and passions	I am focused on my own needs, interests, and passions in the light of what I perceive to be the needs of my organization	I am focused on interests or passions that I care about and also fill a need in my organization	I am focused on building personal capacity that seamlessly meshes my interests and passions with the needs of my organization

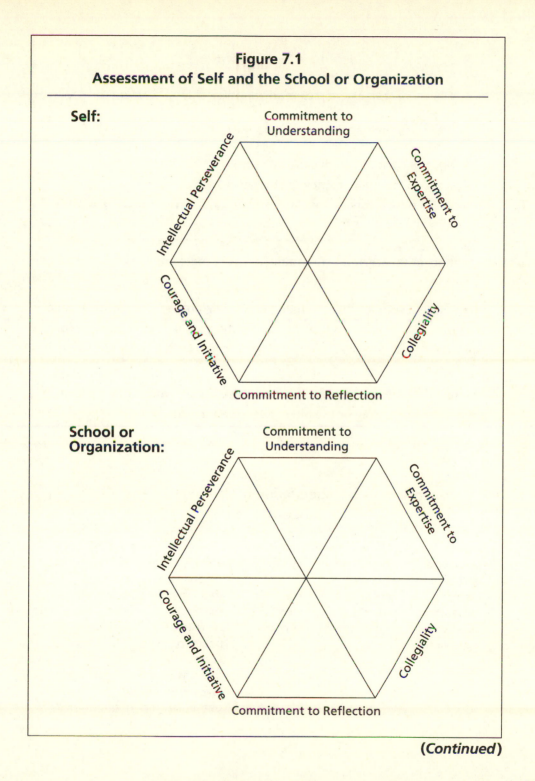

Figure 7.1
Assessment of Self and the School or Organization

Self:

Commitment to Understanding

Intellectual Perseverance

Commitment to Expertise

Courage and Initiative

Collegiality

Commitment to Reflection

School or Organization:

Commitment to Understanding

Intellectual Perseverance

Commitment to Expertise

Courage and Initiative

Collegiality

Commitment to Reflection

(Continued)

1. When you look at the picture of your dispositions, what does it say to you?
2. When you look at the picture you drew of the organization's dispositions, what does it make you think?
3. What of what you see is okay with you?
4. What do think you might want to change? Why?
5. Which of the dispositions is most important for you to cultivate within this organization? Why?

participation in the learning community. This is the completed list of baseline requirements:

- Application revealing ability to reflect on professional practice in the form of a letter, a video, or other media. The application should reveal the applicant's motivation for becoming a fellow and his or her expectations of the fellowship experience.
- Statement describing what the applicant values as an educator in the form of a philosophy of learning or teaching or a vision for schools.

Table 7.2
Commitment to Understanding: Use of Data and Work, Student Version

---

| Use of relevant and pertinent data and evidence in work and argumentation | I know how smart I am in a subject because of the grades that I get | I can look at my work and tell what I still need to work on | I use my work as well as the feedback that I get from my teacher and peers to know what needs work and to figure out a plan for improving | I use my work and my teachers' lessons and assignments to figure out what I need to do; then I use my next piece of work to see if what I tried is working |

- Two letters of recommendation, one of which is written by a supervisor. The other letter could be replaced with an observation that documents the applicant's strengths or talents.

- Learning experience or work sample of best practice that shows the applicant's experience or achievements in teaching and learning with an accompanying reflection.

- Résumé that includes evidence of participation in or facilitation of learning.

Several of the individual measures in this book can be used to foster a continuous exploration of community members' thinking and work by having them examine and articulate the ways in which they cultivate the dispositions of practice through the use of evidence that stems from their work activities. This is no easy feat since these dispositions represent abiding tendencies, beliefs, and values that are not always transparent. Providing compelling evidence of their possession of a disposition is far more difficult than claiming status on the basis of a degree, role, or position or claiming expertise on the basis of activities undertaken and events that can be listed and counted.

Over two years, we have collaboratively developed and refined several checklists and rubrics to help participants in professional learning communities assess and document the development of these dispositions. Participants refer to these tools on a regular basis. The community uses them as part of the induction process of new participants in the community, to deepen everyone's understanding of the values and behaviors it upholds, and as part of assessing their overall attainment in the community.

To collect evidence of their growth and attainment of the dispositions, community members can score themselves for each disposition by selecting one of the following descriptors:

- I do not understand what this disposition is and cannot see a connection to my work.

- I am learning about this disposition and have set goals to practice it in my work.

- I am developing this disposition and exhibit it in some parts of my work.

- I regularly and consistently practice this disposition throughout my work.

- I exemplify this disposition and consciously work to help others develop it, too.

Following their selection, community members identify evidence to support their selection and describe it in writing as they ponder the question: What led you to your assessment? Exhibit 7.1 illustrates this measure as it applies to Commitment to Reflection.

Any of the individual assessments can be used as a learning opportunity for community members to learn about and from each other. This would be the case if, during one of the first meetings, the facilitator asked participants to share their data related to their lowest- and highest-scoring disposition. Following is an excerpt of the self-assessment process as it relates to Commitment to Reflection, which was produced as a result of using the self-assessment in Exhibit 7.3:

Developing

One of my goals is to develop my capacity to be a reflective practitioner. In an attempt to do so, I have started to incorporate reflective processes and activities into my major activities. Right now I am developing a "Reflective Toolbox" that includes the following items:

- Behavior-over-time chart for all the professional development programs I participate in
- Reflective questions I use with teachers, students, and myself when I formally present any materials
- Reflective essays I complete at the beginning and end of the school year
- Reflective logs I use after completing any formal peer review

This self-assessment is accompanied by evidence that includes some of the completed items on the preceding list. This helps ground the self-assessment process in a concrete artifact or object, process, or event, allowing it to be shared both within and outside the community.

Another strategy for promoting the exploration and engagement with the dispositions of practice through the discussion of evidence entails asking individuals to identify questions that, when answered, lead to the illustration and annotation of work-related artifacts around the dispositions of practice and their embodiment. Our process for helping community members

Exhibit 7.1
Commitment to Reflection: Self-Assessment

REFLECTIVITY

Using an awareness of your own thinking and learning as a way to assess and understand yourself, work, and the organization; identifying goals, actions, and strategies needed to make changes or decisions or produce work

Prereadiness	Beginning	Developing	Deepening	Embodying
I do not understand what this disposition is and cannot see a connection to my work.	I am learning about this disposition and have set goals to practice it in my work.	I am developing this disposition and exhibit it in some of my work.	I regularly and consistently practice this disposition throughout my work.	I exemplify this disposition and consciously work to help others develop it too.

Possible Evidence: Self-assessment

Response to a peer assessment

Identification of patterns, trends, interdependencies, and consequences

Rationales for projects, units, programs, and so forth

Explanation of the thinking that leads to stated goals and/or action plans

Your Evidence: What led you to your above assessment? Please provide examples to support and illustrate your thinking.

generate questions that would help them provide evidence of the dispositions is included below.

Participants work in pairs or triads through three stages of work. In Stage 1, Drafting, they select a disposition and generate two or three questions whose answers would reveal the extent to which a person evidences such disposition. The questions they generate have to be open-ended, requiring an explicit connection between the disposition's descriptor and an individual, demanding answers that are supported by examples or descriptive evidence, and resulting in rich portrayals of the individual's thinking and work.

Sample Questions for Disciplined Inquiry

• What research and data drive the work I do?

• How do data and research inform my day-to-day thinking and work?

• When and how do I seek multiple perspectives on my work?

In Stage 2, Feedback and Refinement, each individual finds another pair or triad to work with to review and refine each other's questions. Once they have revised their questions, they write each question on a strip of paper and post it on the wall, under the chart paper listing the disposition it belongs to. After visiting the posted questions, individuals refine the questions by leaving sticky notes with feedback in the form of comments and questions. In small groups, they review the questions and feedback related to one disposition and make needed revisions.

In Stage 3, Answering Questions, they individually select a disposition and answer the list of refined questions. They also reflect on their use of the questions by addressing the following prompts:

• Which of the questions posted was the easiest for you to respond to?

• Which of the questions was the most difficult for you to address?

• Which questions reveal the most about the extent to which you embody a disposition?

This process enables community members to deepen their understanding of the dispositions of practice while enabling them to articulate questions about them that they understand and own. Following is a list of questions generated by a group of fellows around the disposition of Intellectual Perseverance:

- In what ways do I exhibit that I am flexible and open-minded?
- How have I used the feedback I received from others to improve my work?
- How does my work support and enhance my organization?
- What are the standards I use to evaluate my work, and how do I know I have met them?
- In what ways does my work push others to learn and grow?

The following reflection by Kathy Perry, a retired art teacher who is currently laying the groundwork for the development of a professional learning community in her former district, provides an illustration of this process and of the dispositions of Intellectual Perseverance and Collegiality:

> I found the process of generating questions for the annotation of the dispositions very helpful. . . . This forced me to see the importance and power of a group effort and thinking. The more one works on something with others, the richer the work becomes, the more familiar one becomes with it, and the deeper one understands it.

MEASURES OF INDIVIDUAL CONTRIBUTIONS TO THE COMMUNITY

In addition to generating questions for the dispositions, participants in learning communities can engage in collaborative work around the annotation of artifacts or work samples that can be used to show evidence of their attainment. Such evidence can be used to strengthen the community and its supporting organization.

In a shared annotation process, participants work in pairs. They first exchange artifacts with their partner. After carefully examining their partner's artifact, they identify its context by answering the following questions:

- What is the artifact? What is its intended purpose?
- Who produced the artifact?
- Who is the intended audience?

They then identify the artifact's connection to the dispositions of practice by pondering the following questions:

- Which disposition of practice and its specific manifestations does the artifact exemplify?
- How does it do that?
- At what level?

They then use the rubric in Appendix A to score the dispositions that they see a connection to. They identify the specific excerpts, sections, quotations, or segments of the artifact that evidence the disposition and respond to the guiding questions that would provide the most compelling evidence of the author's possession of the disposition.

For teachers, artifacts may include drafts and revisions of lessons, assessments, and units, coupled with samples of student work. For students, they may include written essays, reflections, and projects. For administrators, they may include budgets, grant proposals, action plans, written studies, and analysis of past programs or policies. Artifacts that professional developers could use may include program plans, reflective analysis of teachers' work resulting from a program they taught, action research write-ups, or course designs. University faculty might use courses, analysis of student work resulting from a program, assessments, or program designs.

The collaborative work around the annotation of artifacts benefits the community in at least two ways. First, it serves as a learning opportunity around the dispositions that the community is trying to foster. Second, it helps community members identify artifacts that strengthen the work of the community and the organization so that they can document their growth and attainment in terms of these dispositions.

Diana Feige, a university professor, illustrates the use and value of the annotation process. The artifact she selected was a class assignment in which undergraduate students were asked to identify and bring a metaphor or object that described their evolution and growth as learners and future teachers during the semester. The metaphor or object was to be accompanied by a two- to three-page reflective narrative that articulated how it captured the essence of their growth. Diana identified her classroom assignment as evidence of her cultivation of a Commitment to Reflection given that it required that students reflect on their learning and the value of reflection.

After examining the rubric and discussing the artifact with another fellow, Diana realized that the artifact itself lacked the kind of elaboration or explanation that would make her intentions and values explicit and had this to say: "I self-assess as a 'Developing Level' being that this, as a stand alone, does not account for how consistently reflection is a part of the course or embedded in students' learning, in the work they do, or in how I use it to inform my thinking." To strengthen the rating for this artifact, Diana would have had to include the specific reflective prompts explicitly connected to her assignment that scaffolded student reflection. This example illustrates how the collaborative annotation led to a reexamination of the assumptions surrounding the evidence of the disposition in a particular artifact.

Theresa Gray is a staff developer who recently analyzed one of her work samples for evidence of Commitment to Reflection. This sample was a printout of a blog she created for individuals who teach, read, or investigate writing. She wrote the following reflection:

> I am honestly not sure that I am looking for patterns in the feedback I am receiving from the people that interact with my blog! I am really looking for people to ask questions back, challenge my thinking, and in general, share their reflections. I do include what I notice about workshop participants' evaluation in my building, so I guess I search for patterns in that feedback, as it usually forms the basis for my blog!

Theresa's interaction with the artifact and its subsequent annotation using the rubric led her to explicitly describe the desired outcomes for the artifact to identify patterns, something she had not thought about before.

In addition to assessing the dispositions of practice through the annotation of work samples, participants may develop a learner portfolio to document their work inside the community. The example of a portfolio framework in Table 7.3 was guided by reconciling a set of reflective questions with the work that community members had done in the community over a three-year period.

Community members may also create showcase or certification portfolios when they have produced tangible evidence of high attainment of the dispositions of practice. These portfolios provide participants with formal opportunities

Table 7.3
Portfolio Framework with Reflection Questions

Possible Artifacts or Work Samples	Reflection Questions
Unit, lesson or activity, or action research that illustrates practices before this program	What does this work show about my strengths before this program? What does it show about my needs?
Revision to unit, lesson or activity, or action research designed before this program that incorporates learning from this year	How has my practice changed? What am I doing differently or to a lesser or greater extent?
Work developed after one of the four program days prior to the summer	What does this work show about my strengths? What does it show about my needs?
Work developed in the summer	What does this unit show about my strengths and weaknesses as a curriculum writer? What does this unit show about my growth in this program?
Goals identified at the end of the summer session or the beginning of the year	Why were those goals important? How do I feel about those goals now? What will change in my practice or work as a result of achieving these goals?
End-of-year reflection	What does this reflection show about what matters to me? How would I describe myself in terms of my reflectivity?
Beginning-of-year reflection	What do I want to accomplish this year? Why is that important? What will change in my practice or work as a result of achieving these goals? How do I see myself as a professional?
Analysis of professional strengths and weaknesses	What are my strengths as a teacher, designer, assessor, learner? What are my needs as a teacher, designer, assessor, learner?

to self-assess and judge their work through the lens of the dispositions. They also provide the larger community with opportunities to learn more about their dispositions and their manifestations and use them as exemplars for new members.

To demonstrate their overall attainment as participants in the professional learning community, fellows in one of our professional learning communities used a certification or showcase rubric to complete a certification portfolio. The portfolio is reviewed internally by staff and by an external panel of practitioners, administrators, and university faculty who serve as critical friends to the fellow and also function as an outside advisory group for the community.

Table 7.4 includes an excerpt of the certification rubric related to Intellectual Perseverance. Once again, notice the identification of evidence, this time in the portfolio. This promotes deeper thinking around each disposition and limits the degree to which claims about attainment go unsubstantiated, thereby lending rigor to the assessment measure.

The primary value of the tools and processes described in this chapter lies in their usability to assess, monitor, and identify new and improved actions and processes for the community and its members. In a sense, they are both assessment tools and mechanisms to ensure the quality and viability of the work that participants in the learning community value and seek to preserve.

Table 7.4
Certification Portfolio: Intellectual Perseverance

Process: *What does this disposition looks like when practiced?*	1	2	3	4
Willingness to change and improve own thinking and work and/or to pursue an idea or question for a period of time; continuous revisiting of own work; withholding need to resolve or finish work before its time; commitment to improving own organization, and to the completion of work to publicly held standards.	Committed to own suppositions based on faith and own perspective as if it were fixed. More likely to impose ideas on others than to listen to others' ideas. Unquestioningly sacrifices own perspectives and beliefs based on other opinions or committed to own perspectives and beliefs as if fixed.	Unquestioningly sacrifices own suppositions and perspective based on others' opinions. Is willing to hear others' perspectives and beliefs, but is unsure about merging them with own ideas.	Is aware and able to articulate own perspective and beliefs while being flexible and open to change.	Is aware and able to articulate own perspectives and beliefs and is open-minded, flexible, and intellectually humble in ways that others seek to emulate.
	Has a hard time accepting that a draft of own work needs to be revised to meet highest standard.	Is willing to revise own work to attain highest standard with very little prompting.	Is eager to revise and improve work to attain highest standard without any prompting.	Is committed to revising own work, never assuming that the last revision made is the final one; eager to reach highest external standard.
	Is interested in satisfying own professional interests and needs.	Is interested in entertaining organizational needs and trying to reconcile them with own work.	Seeks to address organizational needs with own work.	Seeks to improve own organization and is willing to direct and tailor own work toward that end.

Portfolio evidence: What is revealed in the portfolio artifacts that show this disposition?	Portfolio includes documents/artifacts that reveal:	Portfolio includes documents/artifacts that reveal:	Portfolio includes documents/artifacts that reveal:	Portfolio includes documents/artifacts that reveal:
	• Work in first draft or initial format • Work that reflects the voice and opinions of an outside reader or a perspective that is contrary to best practice • Work that reflects own interests	• Work that represents revisions based on someone else's input • Revision of work based on self-assessment using established criteria for quality from product rubrics • Work that reflects an attempt to reconcile own interests with those of own organization	• Revision of work based on implementation and analysis of data collected from implementation • Assessment and revision of work using feedback from multiple peer review and editorial reviews • Work that reflects a clear alignment between own work and the interests of own organization	• Multiple revisions of work based on new learning from research and outside sources • Assessment and revision of work based on implementation and analysis of data collected from implementation, feedback from multiple peer review and editorial reviews, and input from own organization • Explicit statements acknowledging the "imperfections" of the work and an interest and/or commitment to its continued revision • Work that reflects a clear and explicit attempt to address important organizational goals

What Is the Promise of Professional Learning Communities?

Everyone involved in teaching and learning has had moments of deep understanding, insight, innovation, and inspiration. These moments, if unpacked and understood, have the potential to enrich teachers and other practitioners whose lives revolve around schools. Professional learning communities are the contexts that cultivate those moments and allow its members to string them together to tell powerful stories.

Professional learning communities can develop the space for people to operate as learners. They can create opportunities for their members to articulate their tacit knowledge and understandings and internalize the day-to-day insights that are derived from their work. Such articulation, if mediated by structures that promote deep and meaningful discourse, can produce new shared knowledge and understandings that build the capacity of the individuals and the group to improve on their practices and work to see the big picture rather than isolated events and problems, and to address respectfully the challenges imposed by tapping everyone's learning potential.

Professional learning communities can provide the structures and processes that support learning while doing, responsive rather than reactive behaviors, and the capability of making informed decisions about curriculum priorities. They can foster mechanisms for members to develop a clear and transparent vision of their school, assume a shared purpose, and pursue together the work of making their organization a worthy setting for teaching and learning. They can create the conditions for teachers, alone or in groups, to select from myriad educational objectives those that are most pertinent for a specific unit or lesson. They can foster opportunities for principals to develop the leadership capacity of other adults within the school and, in so doing, assume a shared responsibility for schools' processes and outcomes. Finally, they can model collaborative and coherent structures that allow students to see themselves as part of a larger whole and understand that their learning is not just theirs.

In the absence of such communities, we resign ourselves to believing in magical moments as merely isolated moments in time to be enjoyed only by those who witness them: a teacher's explanation led to students' insight and understanding, a principal's goal-setting process encouraged teachers to believe and maximize their potential, and a staff developer's activity inspired a veteran teacher who had not deviated from her practice in ten years to try and ultimately implement a new and powerful strategy to engage her students. In the absence of professional learning communities, we relinquish the opportunity to watch a teacher and other practitioners devote the time, energy, and thoughtfulness to create assessments, programs, and studies for no other reason than to make a contribution to the profession. We forgo the opportunity to unify students, teachers, parents, university faculty, professional developers, and school and district administrators in the quest to make a difference in the lives of teachers and students.

We let go of the idea that people who devote their professional lives to schools and who work closest to children cannot make an important contribution to school improvement.

Some of the most innovative and responsive companies have a research and development division and devote significant portions of their operating expenses to research and inquiry. Some of them create formal creativity silos, where individuals can rescind the day-to-day operating procedures and policies so they can be free to think creatively. Many of them routinely encourage collaborations across divisions and departments and expose their staff to all kinds of experiences that enable them to look at their organization from a global perspective, while considering problems and issues in need of attention. Why is this not part of the world of schools?

Every school and district in this country should have one or more professional learning communities that conduct research and development work, while at the same time preserving the social intelligence amassed by practitioners and learners.

Close to one hundred years of failed attempts at educational reform in this country should provide us with enough evidence that externally driven approaches to improving the educational system do not produce schools that function as learning organizations. It is time that we believe that practice, experience, and expertise can greatly inform the actions, practices, policies, and programs that schools and other educational organizations can use to make schools places that honor learning for everyone.

We now know how professional learning communities vary, much as other organizations do, but they all support teaching and learning. We have ample evidence that the outcomes of professional learning communities are deliberate and thoughtful products and processes that enrich the lives of school inhabitants. We have learned much about assessing and developing individual and organizational readiness for supporting learning communities. We have gained significant insights from the roles, responsibilities, and activities of individuals and groups who participate in all kinds of learning communities. We are learning more and more but have much to learn about how to develop communities that can sustain their work and the community as a structure over time.

We need professional learning communities because all the adults who operate within schools should take their own expertise and thinking seriously enough to merit scrutiny and use their professional judgments along with their knowledge and skills to help students learn and value such learning. We need these communities because schools are complex systems that house adults and children who are multifaceted beings. Such complexity deserves more than the too common hierarchical and segmented organization of schools and professional roles.

The promise of professional learning communities lies in its potential to harness the expertise of individuals who are vested in the improvement of adult and student learning. Whereas individuals and communities can engage in all kinds of activities depending on the specific focus of the learning community, their work should support student, adult, and organizational learning and connect individual interests with organizational goals.

Imagine if everyone in a school thought that what happened in every classroom, to every teacher and every student, was of tremendous significance and that quality learning was the most valued commodity. What would that mean for how time is used? What would it enable in terms of teachers' interactions with others? What would principals, teachers, and community members believe in and expect? What would students be able to accomplish?

What are we waiting for?

Rubric for Assessing Individual Capacity for Professional Learning Communities

Commitment to Understanding: Pursuing questions and developing ideas related to teaching and learning, accessing multiple perspectives, and using research and evidence

	Beginning — Commitment to Understanding May Be Present But Is Unrecognized	Developing — Commitment to Understanding Appears Inconsistently	Deepening — Commitment to Understanding Is Recognized and Becoming Important	Embodying — Commitment to Understanding Is Integrated Throughout
Discourse — Pursuing questions and developing ideas related to teaching and learning	Repeats questions that others raise Questions are numerous, general, and/or unfocused Admits to recognizing names of important figures or movements in education, past or present	Identifies and pursues others' questions to focus own inquiry Questions are specific to a topic but may not deepen understanding Reads articles and research on education and responds to questions if provided by someone else	Raises and pursues own questions to increase learning and/or explore own and others' assumptions Questions are focused and deepen understanding of a topic or lead to new questions Reads and refers to research and theories about teaching and learning in planned discussions	Questions and raises issues that challenge the status quo and demand a reexamination of deeply held assumptions Questions target a gap in the current research on a specific topic and lead to new, pertinent questions Seeks, updates, and uses research and theories in conversations and own practice
Behavior and Practice — Accessing multiple perspectives	Agrees in principle that other legitimate perspectives exist, but allocates them little credence in practice Sacrifices own perspective based on opinions of others; or immovable in own perspective and beliefs	Is willing to hear others' perspectives and beliefs, but unsure about merging them with own Is willing to be influenced by others' perspectives on value-laden issues	Actively explores perspectives of others when presented in order to broaden own perspective Maintains own perspectives and beliefs while being flexible and open to change	Seeks out and learns from perspectives of others to challenge and revisit own perspective Promotes own perspectives and beliefs while appreciating those of others
Work — Using research and evidence	Work is grounded primarily in personal experiences and own opinion Work incorporates conclusions in the absence of specific evidence	Work reflects a cursory attention to others' perspectives and is supported by limited evidence of work Work includes data from a single source to ascertain learning needs	Work is anchored in multiple perspectives and research Work uses data from several sources or measures to determine and discuss learning needs and identify ideas for strategies to meet those needs	Work reflects a careful integration of own experience, grounded understandings, varied evidence, and informed research Work incorporates the use of multiple and different data sources and evidence to surface problems and issues or to test assumptions and inferences related to learning

Intellectual Perseverance: Considering ideas or questions for a period of time to improve our work; revising and revisiting our work and our thinking to improve it and to reach high standards; and withholding the need to finish work before it is the best that it can be

	Beginning Intellectual Perseverance May Be Present But Is Unrecognized	*Developing* Intellectual Perseverance Appears Inconsistently	*Deepening* Intellectual Perseverance Is Recognized and Becoming Important	*Embodying* Intellectual Perseverance Is Integrated Throughout
Discourse Considering ideas or questions for a period of time to improve our work	Asserts that others may need time to revise work, but believes that own work is fine as is Entertains ideas or questions for the moment, but is constantly distracted by other topics of interest or perceived importance	Willing to discuss the possibility that own thinking or a draft of own work may need to be revised Considers ideas or questions when raised by others and engaged in a formal conversation, but will return to them only if required	Discusses with colleagues own ideas for revisions to own thinking or work Discusses own and others' ideas or questions formally or informally, and returns willingly to those that relate to own needs and interests	Solicits feedback from others on own thinking and work in order to revise and improve it Engages colleagues and others in ongoing debates and conversations about questions and ideas that challenge current beliefs and practices
Behavior and Practice Revising and revisiting our work and our thinking to improve it and to reach high standards	Focuses on satisfying own professional interests and needs Frustrated by an expectation to revise	Recognizes others' needs and tries to reconcile them with own interests and work Tolerates the notion of revision in order for the work to be finished	Addresses others' needs through own interests and work Eager to revise and improve own thinking and work in the moment to meet a standard	Reconciles own interests and work with the needs of others and of own organization Committed to the ongoing revision of own thinking and work to reach the highest standards
Work Withholding the need to finish work before it's the best that it can be	End product is virtually the same as the original draft Uses time provided for revision to accomplish other tasks	Identifies needed revisions to own work Revises own thinking and work within time provided by those expecting the revisions	Revises thinking and work to correct perceived problems Finds or makes the time necessary to revise own thinking and work	Rethinks or revises own thinking, producing multiple drafts of improved work Revises own thinking and work on a continuous basis, even when faced with impending deadlines or fatigue

Courage and Initiative: Discussing uncomfortable topics or issues, including own values and questions; accepting the discomfort that stems from the need to change; seeking or accepting new or unfamiliar roles, responsibilities, or challenges

	Beginning Courage and Initiative May Be Present But Are Unrecognized	*Developing* Courage and Initiative Appear Inconsistently	*Deepening* Courage and Initiative Are Recognized and Becoming Important	*Embodying* Courage and Initiative Are Integrated Throughout
Discourse Discussing uncomfortable topics or issues, including own values and questions	Shares values and assumptions when asked but does not tie them to actions	Shares values and assumptions during activities in which that is expected	Shares values and assumptions openly and ties them to actions	Shares values and assumptions to play devil's advocate and stimulate discourse
	Hesitates to ask for clarification or asks questions only when prompted directly	Asks questions but only when others have done so first	Asks questions that reveal the limits of own understanding	Asks questions that reveal own limitations and helps others do the same
	Articulates issues or questions about teaching and learning that require no discussion	Attends planned discussions of issues or questions about teaching and learning but participates only in terms of agreeing or disagreeing	Articulates beliefs and questions about teaching and learning in conversations and discussions	Articulates beliefs and questions about teaching and learning, even when they are unresolved, difficult, or may make others uncomfortable
Behavior and Practice Accepting the discomfort that stems from the need to change	Stays away from people who appear to be unlike her or him or from activities that may create dissonance	Listens to people or activities that may create dissonance but does not actively engage with them	Is comfortable with dissonance and seeks to resolve it, even if it requires hard work	Welcomes cognitive dissonance and pursues new understandings
	Avoids sharing own work or thinking or apologizes before sharing any work	Shares work and ideas but only after almost everyone in the group has done so	Shares completed and unfinished work openly when opportunities are presented	Shares work, ideas, and questions at any stage of development to seek clarification, improvement, or resolution
	Looks to "superiors" for answers to issues or problems to determine what to do	Seeks guidance from others in achieving resolution of issues and problems in an effort to promote harmony	Actively pursues resolution of issues and problems in an effort to reduce conflict or tension	Actively pursues insights and resolution to issues and problems, even if such pursuit produces conflict or dissent
Work Seeking or accepting new or unfamiliar roles, responsibilities, or challenges	Maintains current position or responsibilities even when they are not challenging	Accepts new roles or responsibilities but is hesitant and uncomfortable with this change	Seeks and accepts new responsibilities and is interested in learning from them	Actively seeks new challenges, roles, and responsibilities as a way of staying energized
	Work and ideas are within what is accepted or expected	Work and ideas define what is accepted or expected	Work and ideas raise questions of what is accepted or expected	Work and ideas challenge what is accepted or expected

Commitment to Reflection: Sharing our thinking to develop and evaluate it; thinking about our thinking and learning in order to set goals, assess and understand ourselves, our work, and our organization; producing work that results from goals, actions, and strategies that are grounded in the analysis of past learning

	Beginning Commitment to Reflection May Be Present But Is Unrecognized	*Developing* Commitment to Reflection Appears Inconsistently	*Deepening* Commitment to Reflection Is Recognized and Becoming Important	*Embodying* Commitment to Reflection Is Integrated Throughout
Discourse Sharing our thinking to develop and evaluate it	Needs guiding questions or prompts to express own thinking about self and work Speaks guardedly about questions related to own work and thinking	Assesses own work during formal reflective opportunities Speaks openly about questions related to own work and thinking	Articulates the meaning and value of own work on a regular basis during formal reflective opportunities and in conversations initiated by others Speaks thoughtfully about questions related to own work and thinking, connecting them to possible actions	Asks questions about own practice and assesses value of own thinking and work independently and continuously Illustrates the impact of own thinking and questions about work
Behavior and Practice Thinking about our thinking and learning in order to set goals, assess, and understand ourselves, our work, and our organization	Arbitrarily sets narrow, disjointed targets or broad idealistic goals Acknowledges a connection between own thinking and quality or merit of work Considers possible actions related to own work in terms of how difficult they might be to implement	Articulates general goals peripherally connected to self-assessment Identifies general strengths and weaknesses in own work and thinking Considers possible actions related to own work in terms of how they relate to improving that work	Articulates carefully thought-out, realistic goals Assesses strengths and weaknesses of own thinking and work in terms of their impact on self and others Considers possible actions related to own work in terms of how they might move them toward their goals	Identifies strategic goals and indicators Assesses own thinking and work in terms of their role and contributions to self, others, and own organization Considers possible actions related to own work in terms of their unintended and intended consequences
Work Producing work that results from goals, actions, and strategies grounded in the analysis of past learning	Acknowledges that patterns, trends, interdependencies, and consequences exist in the work of others Identifies general areas in need of improvement related to own work	Recognizes patterns, trends, consequences, and interdependencies when pointed out Identifies specific areas for improvement connected to an assessment of own work	Searches for patterns, trends, consequences, and interdependencies in their own thinking and work Identifies specific areas and strategies for improvement that connect to an assessment of their current reality and work	Uses their understanding and recognition of patterns, trends, consequences, and interdependencies to assess and adjust own thinking and work Identifies and prioritizes specific areas for improvement, with supporting strategies based on a careful assessment of impact on current work or organization

Commitment to Expertise: Refining and expanding our current professional knowledge and skills; disseminating our knowledge and expertise within and outside our own organization; engaging in learning and work that addresses organizational or professional needs

	Beginning Commitment to Expertise May Be Present But Is Unrecognized	*Developing* Commitment to Expertise Appears Inconsistently	*Deepening* Commitment to Expertise Is Recognized and Becoming Important	*Embodying* Commitment to Expertise Is Integrated Throughout
Discourse Refining and expanding our current professional knowledge and skills	Researches an assigned question or area of focus Seeks to work with existing knowledge and skills base	Engages in individual research and discussion of an area of interest Seeks to add to existing knowledge and skills base	Engages in learning and inquiry experiences to answer questions and deepen understanding Seeks to "perfect" existing knowledge and skills base	Engages in individual and collaborative action research and professional learning experiences to help others learn, as well as improve own understanding and practice Seeks to acquire new skills and knowledge to augment and complement knowledge and practice
Behavior and Practice Disseminating our knowledge and expertise within and outside our own organization	Recognizes that learning and improvement are needed Dreads the idea of presenting own work Is hesitant to acknowledge learning, experiences, expertise	Realizes that learning is still needed but circumscribes such learning to predetermined time slots Views presenting or sharing own work as an obligation Is willing to share learning, experiences, and expertise with peers	Sees self primarily as a learner and has difficulty explicitly acknowledging expertise that could be shared Views presenting own work, formally or informally, as a responsibility Is willing to share learning, experiences, and expertise with colleagues who share roles and responsibilities	Recognizes own expertise but acknowledges its limitations and proactively seeks additional learning Holds presenting at conference days or in other public forums as a personal expectation rather than a duty Makes explicit efforts to share learning, experiences, and expertise with others, within and beyond own work setting
Work Engaging in learning and work that addresses organizational or professional needs	Focuses on satisfying own professional interests and needs Attends required learning programs, collaborative study groups, collegial circles, action research experiences	Recognizes others' needs and tries to reconcile them with own interests and work Participates, if invited, in learning programs, self-defined study groups, collegial circles, and action research about own work	Addresses others' needs through own interests and work Initiates and engages in individual and collaborative action research and in learning programs that relate to own and others' work	Reconciles own interests and work with the needs of others and of own organization Initiates, designs, and facilitates inquiry and professional development experiences that deepen own and others' work

Collegiality: Learning with and from others; acting on the belief that learning and working with others increases our expertise, producing work that results from engaging in collaborative learning and problem solving

	Beginning Collegiality May Be Present But Is Unrecognized	Developing Collegiality Appears Inconsistently in Discourse, Behavior, and Work	Deepening Collegiality Present, Recognized, and Becoming Important	Embodying Collegiality Integrated into Discourse, Behavior, and Work
Discourse Learning with and from others	Discusses own practices with others when required	Participates in discussions related to own practices when invited	Seeks out opportunities to explore and discuss own and best practices	Helps self and others discuss, understand, develop, and articulate best practices
Behavior and Practice Acting on the belief that learning and working with others increases our expertise	Offers and accepts support when required Knows that colleagues are available to discuss questions and learning, but prefers to think alone	Willingly offers and asks for support during formal exchanges Is curious about what colleagues are doing or trying	Seeks opportunities to offer and ask for support Is interested in learning with and from others	Designs structured opportunities to support shared learning and the work of others Is eager to expand and build on others' work or thinking
Work Producing work that results from collaborative learning and problem solving	Shares own work when asked to Participates in collaborative work when invited to do so but focuses exclusively on own work	Shares own work with others with self-interest in mind Engages in collaborative work spontaneously when such work is directly connected to own needs	Shares own work with others and encourages others to do the same, even if such work does not relate to immediate self-interests Participates and advocates for opportunities for collaborative inquiry and learning	Models the value of sharing and collaboration through the sharing of own work and thinking that supports others' learning Initiates, facilitates, or designs collaborative learning opportunities and projects and seeks to work with others to create new thinking, perspectives, and work

Rubric for Assessing Organizational Capacity for Professional Learning Communities

Commitment to Understanding: Supporting the pursuit of questions and development of ideas related to teaching and learning, valuing multiple perspectives, and using data, research, and evidence

	Beginning Commitment to Understanding May Be Present But Is Unrecognized	*Developing* Commitment to Understanding Appears Inconsistently	*Deepening* Commitment to Understanding Is Recognized and Becoming Important	*Systemic* Commitment to Understanding Is Integrated Throughout
Discourse Supporting the pursuit of questions and development of ideas related to teaching and learning	Consults selected individuals about decisions related to teaching, learning, and organizational development — Publicizes organizational goals	Involves groups of selected individuals in discussions about teaching, learning, and organizational development — Consults groups of selected individuals about the implementation of organizational goals and decisions	Engages mixed-staff groups in conversations around teaching, learning, and organizational development — Promotes discussions about proposed programs, policies, and outcomes at all levels of the organization	Uses horizontal and vertical teams to uncover different perspectives and address questions about teaching, learning, and organizational development — Dedicates time, space, and resources to support ongoing discussion and analysis of organizational outcomes and to assess whether they are as good as they can be
Behavior and Practice Valuing multiple perspectives	Makes decisions about programs, policies, and practices based on recent experiences and emotions — Reacts to initiative-related problems or issues by attributing responsibility or blame	Refers to past and current experience when making decisions — Responds to initiative-related problems or issues when they arise	Relies on past and current experience, as well as research, in coming to decisions — Monitors initiatives and programs to ensure immediate response to problems and issues should they arise	Considers past and current experiences, needs, and goals, as well as current research, in determining next steps — Slows down and ponders the implementation of initiatives and programs to allow multiple feedback loops
Work Using data, research, and evidence	System for collecting data is in place but used inconsistently across the organization — Data are collected but remain unanalyzed and unused	Data collection system is in place and used consistently — Analysis of data collected is superficial or spotty	Data are consistently and systemically gathered — Collected data are analyzed and used to support organizational decisions	Systems for gathering, using, and responding to data are fluid and consistent — Ongoing analysis of data informs the organization's work

Intellectual Perseverance: Discussing and revisiting work and thinking in order to improve it; using vision and goals to develop and assess the organization; establishing and implementing quality control mechanisms

	Beginning Intellectual Perseverance May Be Present But Is Unrecognized	*Developing* Intellectual Perseverance Appears Inconsistently	*Deepening* Intellectual Perseverance Is Recognized and Becoming Important	*Systemic* Intellectual Perseverance Is Integrated Throughout
Discourse Discussing and revisiting work and thinking in order to improve it	Assumes that the organization's improvement is either an event or the responsibility of a single individual Engages in immediate, full-scale implementation of all initiatives	Provides selected staff with opportunities to discuss organizational improvement efforts Programs, policies, and practices are defined and implemented by a selected group	Has a process and structure in place for organizational improvement and uses it to assess the organization Programs, policies, and practices are defined, implemented, and refined with input from various levels of the organization	Uses and regularly evaluates strategic processes and structures to support the continuous improvement of the organization Programs, policies, and practices are defined, implemented, and refined through a process including multiple cycles of field testing, feedback, and revision from individuals at various levels of the organization
Behavior and Practice Using vision and goals to develop and assess the organization	Claims to have an organizational vision but keeps it private Establishes multiple, unrelated goals	Identifies the organization's vision and makes it public Announces several related or unrelated goals and priorities and asks staff to think of ways to support them	Links the organization's vision to programs and policies Identifies several related long-term goals and priorities, making connections between these goals and specific endeavors of the organization	Uses the organization's vision as a compass for decision making Commits to limited goals and priorities over an extended period of time, aligning organizational endeavors with staff's work and evaluation of specific goals
Work Establishing and implementing quality control mechanisms	Programs, policies, and practices are drafted and implemented by one or more individuals Expects goal achievement and "check ups" through unannounced observation or impromptu written reports	Moves from recommendations to large-scale implementation Periodically gathers feedback on the extent to which the organization's goals and priorities are being addressed	Researches thoroughly before large-scale implementation Regularly provides time for discussion and updates on the extent to which the organization's goals and priorities are being addressed	Routinely field-tests before piloting and pilots before large-scale implementation Routinely and explicitly engages multiple perspectives in conversation about the degree to which goals and priorities are being addressed and implemented

Courage and Initiative: Enabling the consideration and discussion of uncomfortable topics or issues; accepting the discomfort that stems from the need to change; embracing challenges and innovations

	Beginning Courage and Initiative May Be Present But Are Unrecognized	*Developing* Courage and Initiative Appear Inconsistently in Discourse, Behavior, and Work	*Deepening* Courage and Initiative Are Recognized and Becoming Important	*Systemic* Courage and Initiative Are Integrated Throughout
Discourse Enabling the consideration of uncomfortable topics or issues	Promotes the expectation that if conflicts or issues surface, they are taken care of quietly and privately Ignores or strives to stifle dissenting voices	Provides opportunity for members of the organization to explore differences of opinion when they occur Monitors conversations airing individual or organizational differences carefully to be sure they do not go "too far"	Develops structures and norms that provide safety to talk about conflicts or problems as they arise Encourages debate of individual and organizational values and assumptions	Incorporates discussion of sensitive issues into daily practice, including skills to broach them with other members of the organization Supports the explicit sharing of different perspectives related to individual and organizational values and assumptions
Behavior and Practice Accepting the discomfort that stems from the need to change	Views situations where there are divergent or conflicting needs as isolated problems to be solved Upholds the belief that conflict is bad and discourages dissenting points of view	Recognizes situations where divergent or conflicting needs must be reconciled as opportunities to acknowledge everyone's needs Values staff members who represent perspectives similar but not necessarily identical to those held by many others	Appreciates divergent or conflicting points of view and seeks to reconcile them Values staff members who represent perspectives different from those held by many, as long as they are not too far from what is popular	Creates or fosters situations where divergent or conflicting needs emerge, treating them as opportunities to explore and reconcile deeply held values and assumptions Encourages and values staff members who represent perspectives different from those held by most, even if unpopular
Work Embracing challenges and innovations	Process is in place for monitoring reactions to implemented organizational changes Innovations are permitted as long as they do not require additional organizational resources or cause complaints from within or outside the organization	Systems are in place for gathering feedback related to proposed organizational innovations Innovations are supported as long as they do not deviate too far from what is accepted or expected and accomplish something perceived to be needed by the organization	Opportunities are created for shared conversations around organizational innovations or changes Innovation around educational questions or needs is encouraged, and resources are provided to support that work	Supports a culture and climate that encourage innovation at all levels of the organization Promoting innovative spirit is an organizational commitment supported by dedicated time, space, and resources

Commitment to Reflection: Valuing shared thinking as a way to develop and evaluate the organization; supporting self-assessment, monitoring, and strategic thinking processes; producing work that results from goals, actions, and strategies grounded in the analysis of past learning

	Beginning Reflectivity May Be Present But Is Unrecognized	Developing Reflectivity Appears Inconsistently	Deepening Reflectivity Is Recognized and Becoming Important	Systemic Reflectivity Is Integrated Throughout
Discourse Valuing shared thinking as a way to develop and evaluate the organization	Verbally acknowledges importance of reflective thinking, but does not provide opportunities for staff to display it	Provides opportunities for members of the organization to think about and ask questions related to needs	Engages staff members in opportunities to articulate and discuss thinking	Provides ongoing opportunities for staff to ponder and discuss their thinking
Behavior and Practice Supporting self-assessment, monitoring, and strategic thinking processes	Assumes that reflective thinking is either an event or the responsibility of an individual	Provides selected staff with opportunities to reflect on their work and practice	Has a structure and processes in place to encourage reflective thinking for staff	Establishes strategic structures and processes that encourage reflective thinking and practice throughout the organization, and periodically evaluates them
	Attends exclusively to staff compliance in evaluation processes	Conducts a cursory evaluation of staff goals and expects adequate time to be provided for descriptive evaluation of staff	Engages staff in an annual goal-setting, action planning, and review process	Creates opportunities for staff to periodically self-evaluate set goals and define or revise actions based on analysis of work-related data
Work Producing work that results from goals, actions, and strategies grounded in the analysis of past learning	Evaluation system includes time for sharing summative evaluations with those involved	Evaluation system incorporates time for feedback from formative assessments before formal evaluation is completed	Evaluation system incorporates time for self-assessment and discussion of feedback from formative assessments before formal evaluation is begun	Evaluation system has multiple, embedded, and specific time periods set aside for self- or peer assessment and reflection using diagnostic, formative, and summative data
	Achievement of individual goals is part of end-of-year evaluation	Information about degree to which individuals and the organization have worked toward achieving schoolwide goals is part of end-of-year evaluation and reflection	Periodic, informal, and formal conversations and other data (for example, observations, work samples, reflections) enable the progress of individual and organizational goals to be tracked	Uses formal, diagnostic, formative, and summative assessments to measure progress and attainment of individual and organizational goals and identify strategies for improving quality and performance

Commitment to Expertise: Refining and expanding current knowledge and skills; disseminating knowledge and expertise within and outside the organization; supporting learning and work that address organizational or professional needs

	Beginning Commitment to Expertise May Be Present But Is Unrecognized	*Developing* Commitment to Expertise Appears Inconsistently	*Deepening* Commitment to Expertise Is Recognized and Becoming Important	*Systemic* Commitment to Expertise Is Integrated Throughout
Discourse Refining and expanding current knowledge and skills	Provides scattered opportunities for own materials, products, and processes to be presented to staff Limits access and exposure to work and conversations with other organizations	Provides opportunities for own materials, products, and processes to be shared internally for implementation Permits outreach to other organizations provided they are financially beneficial or meet a specific organizational need	Provides opportunities to share own materials, products, and processes and projects for feedback, revision, and implementation Encourages reciprocal relationships with other organizations based on learning and work needs	Encourages staff to present own materials, products, and processes for public scrutiny, field-testing, refinement, and publication Creates or pursues opportunities for collaboration with other organizations
Behavior and Practice Disseminating knowledge and expertise within and outside the organization	Expects copies of handouts or materials to be distributed at existing meetings Believes professional development is a series of self-contained events Strives to maintain the work and learning of its staff members within its own walls	Considers requests from staff to share learning at specific organizational meetings Expects professional development to result in staff able to implement learning attained Willing to share its members' work and learning internally or with selected staff from other organizations, networks, or regions	Encourages staff to present internally as well as at conferences Considers professional development an opportunity for creating trainers Seeks to develop and share the work and learning of with selected staff with other organizations, networks, or regions	Maintains the expectation that staff will present at conferences or in other public forums Treats professional development as an ongoing process to maximize expertise, effectiveness, and efficiency Seeks to formally share the work and learning of a wide variety of its members with other organizations, networks, or region
Work Supporting learning and work that addresses organizational or professional needs	Requires staff to engage in predetermined learning and professional development Files information provided about those who acquire additional certifications and credentials and whose work gets published	Encourages staff members to engage in self-selected learning and professional development Commends those who acquire additional certifications or credentials or are published	Expects all staff to think about their learning and work and identify and pursue learning goals Encourages those who wish to pursue additional certifications, credentials, or opportunities for publication	Provides structured opportunities to develop learning, work, questions; engage in research; create professional portfolios Provides support or incentives for the pursuit of additional certifications, credentials, or opportunities for publication

Collegiality: Supporting learning with and from others; acting on the belief that learning and working with others increase our expertise; producing work that stems from collaborative learning and problem solving

	Beginning Collegiality May Be Present But Is Unrecognized	Developing Collegiality Appears Inconsistently	Deepening Collegiality Is Recognized and Becoming Important	Systemic Collegiality Is Integrated Throughout
Discourse Supporting learning with and from others	Requests responses to posed questions Limits accessibility to professional development to isolated individuals and precludes their ability to share with others	Provides opportunities for discussions of shared questions Expects that those who attend professional development will return to the workplace ready to share handouts and ideas	Invites staff discourse on how to foster conditions for shared problem solving and leadership Encourages teams to attend professional development experiences together and provides time afterward for debriefing and processing	Establishes structures and processes that promote and maintain shared discourse, problem solving, and leadership Promotes professional development experiences for cross-role working groups, providing time and resources necessary to continue to share and deepen their learning
Behavior Acting on the belief that learning and working with others increases our expertise	Calls on a core group of staff members whenever necessary Acknowledges the need for communication and collaboration	Forms committees of like-minded individuals to accomplish necessary work Considers proposals for collaborative structures and projects	Forms committees that include diverse roles to accomplish necessary work or research Supports team configurations, common planning time, and visitations within the organization	Brokers different kinds of relationships to help everyone learn from others by organizing and using varied groupings (by role, responsibility, client, or interest) Promotes activities such as peer coaching and explores different ways of accessing members' expertise and work
Work Producing work that stems from collaborative learning and problem solving to produce work	Relies on limited formal mechanisms to address the needs of staff members Provides introductory information about various collaborative teaching, learning, and work-related concepts and practices to several individuals	Processes in place to engage selected individuals in addressing the needs of specific staff members Encourages selected staff to expand their understanding of particular concepts and practices such as collaborative planning, cofacilitation, and integrated design	Collaborative protocols provide process for analysis of staff members' learning or work Encourages staff to collaborate in the design of programs, policies, and activities such as induction processes, collaborative and integrated design or work, or other organizational projects	Collegial structures are used to ascertain and address staff members' and organizational needs Provides structured opportunities for staff to work together to design and implement activities like cofacilitation and teaming approaches, integrated design, new staff induction, and collaborative research

Appendix B: Organizational Capacity for Professional Learning Communities   **169**

Self-Assessment Survey for Participating in Professional Learning Communities

Directions: In the blank to the left of each set of statements, write the letter of the statement that most accurately expresses your thinking. To help you interpret your responses, see the explanations at the end of the measure.

Focus: Things I am interested in, feel strongly about, or question

___ **1.**

    a. I am only interested in finishing work that I am assigned.

    b. I am interested in learning more about the topics that we study in school.

    c. I would like to be able to learn more about topics that I believe are very important to my classmates and me.

    d. I am interested in using what I think I know in order to help students, teachers, and learning, even if it means more work or time.

___ **2.**

    a. I need to stay focused on what I am required or asked to do, so I don't have time for other interests.

    b. There are lots of things that I am interested in learning more about, but there is never enough time to do everything that I have to do and all of the things I want to do.

c. Certain things really interest me, and I try very hard to find time to learn about and do them.

d. I am most interested in exploring how to change things in ways that make school, and maybe even the rest of life, better for everyone.

___ 3.

a. I mostly keep my questions to myself, or I ask someone I think knows the answer.

b. I have no problem asking questions, but I think there may be more than just the answers I get.

c. There are questions I have that I keep asking because I want to know more about them; I share what I learn and know with others.

d. I have questions about how to help make positive, lasting, and important changes.

Alignment: How I think that what I know and am learning is connected to what my school needs

___ 4.

a. I think that my school really just needs me to obey rules and do my work.

b. Much of what I am interested in learning connects to things that are already happening in our school.

c. I am interested in questions and learning that connect to needs I see in myself and students.

d. The ideas, learning, and questions that I care about are all connected to what I think my school needs.

___ 5.

a. My school and I are interested in my doing what I need to do.

b. I think that learning more will help me do what my school and others expect from me.

c. I can help with activities and ideas that are important to my school by learning about them and sharing what I learn.

d. I want to make good and important changes in my school that will last even if I go to another school.

___ **6.**

a. I see myself as a student in this school who will one day leave and go to another school.

b. I see myself as a part of this school, working to do what I am supposed to do.

c. I see myself as someone in this school who helps others in what they do.

d. I see myself as an important member of the school who helps to keep the school going.

Action: What I plan or hope to be able to do with what I am learning

___ **7.**

a. I hope to be able to get through this year.

b. I would like to use what I learn to get better at what I do.

c. I hope to find ways of sharing what I know with others.

d. I would like to be involved in one or two important things that will help the school become a better place.

___ **8.**

a. I will be happy if I can do what I'm supposed to do.

b. I wish I had the time to be creative and really original.

c. I plan to help others to improve their own learning and work.

d. I hope to be able to do things that will improve our school.

Dispositions

How I show evidence of the dispositions of practice that support professional learning in my work and in myself

- I'm curious and ask a lot of questions so that I can better understand.

- I'm not a quitter; I stick with something, even when it gets very difficult.

- I often volunteer to take on activities that I know may be difficult for me.

- I spend a lot of time thinking about my work and trying to understand myself.

- I want to publish or share my work.
- I love to work on teams that have a goal or project to complete.

___ **9.**

    a. I am not sure what these dispositions are, mean, or look like.

    b. I have a hard time taking any of the sentences seriously.

    c. I can easily find sentences that describe me.

    d. I can find sentences that describe me, and also describe other students I know.

___ **10.**

    a. I can't add more to what I am doing right now, especially not something that I don't really understand, like the sentences.

    b. I think the sentences are interesting, and I would like to learn more about them, as long as that doesn't take too much time from the other things that I want to learn or do.

    c. I am interested in thinking more about how the sentences could affect the ways in which I learn and work with others.

    d. I am interested in what these sentences mean for what we are trying to do in the school.

Vision: How I view the future and my place in it

___ **11.**

    a. I think the future will be a lot like today. I will continue to try to do what I am supposed to do.

    b. I see myself as someone who will use what I learn to become a better person.

    c. I see myself as someone who will use what I learn to help others by sharing information and doing what I can to help with different activities.

    d. I want to do something important for my school, my community and maybe even the world.

___ **12.**

    a. One day I hope to have enough time to do everything I should be doing—and to do it well.

b. One day I can imagine being the best that I can be.

c. One day I can see myself helping groups of people to explore their own questions and ideas.

d. I picture myself spending a lot of time thinking about and making important, positive changes that will last.

Availability: How much time do I have to get involved in more activities?

___ 13.

a. I don't see how to use my time differently.

b. I feel that there isn't enough time to do more, but if I am interested in something, I would like to use something like time in class to learn more.

c. Even though we never have enough time, I will make time to share what I know or have done with others who may be able to use it.

d. I want to help plan how we all use time so that everyone at school can do everything they want to do.

___ 14.

a. I have no time to give during the school day, even if there is something that I am interested in doing.

b. I would be okay if the school's schedule could be changed so I would have time to share what I am interested in.

c. I am willing to give up free time during school to learn, develop, and share.

d. I am willing to use my free time during school to figure out how to make time for everyone to share and learn.

___ 15.

a. I have no time after school to do anything else.

b. I would be okay using time after school to share what I am interested in.

c. I am willing to give up free time after school to learn, develop, and share.

d. I am willing to use my free time after school to figure out how to make time for everyone to share and learn.

SURVEY ANALYSIS

If you selected mostly . . .

a: You are practical and results oriented, determined to do well, but frustrated by the number of things that need your time and attention. There is something stopping you from feeling entirely willing or able to participate in a professional learning community at this time. Other things are more important for you to pay attention to right now, and the idea of participating in a professional learning community may feel like an impossibility or an add-on. Time is important to you, and you aren't sure that you should get involved in anything that doesn't seem directly connected to what you already know you have to do.

If someone could help you see that your participation in a professional learning community would benefit you or your students or would enable you to work more efficiently or be more successful, perhaps you would think about this again.

b: You are aware of pressures and time, but are curious enough that you would not mind learning more about them, especially if they were connected to something of interest to you. Right now, you seem to relate strongly to the experiences of members of a community that learns. While you are cautious about overcommitting, you can see the benefit to learning as part of a group. You enjoy sharing ideas and work and would rather learn with others than work by yourself.

You may see that you know certain things, but you are excited by the idea of learning more and you try to find ways to apply what you learn in your work. With help, you could connect your learning to needs in your school. That would help you feel connected to an even larger group and would make the learning seem more important because it relates to things that are inside and outside your own head.

c: You are an eager learner and like to share what you are learning or know. Time is an important concern, but you are sure that you can find or make the time that is necessary to learn and help others learn. You seek out people you believe could benefit from something that you have discovered or are working on. Participation in the community that leads is indicated by the responses that you selected.

Although you might not describe yourself as an expert, you know that there are things you understand that could be helpful to others and would improve your school if only you could share them. You communicate well, and people enjoy learning from and with you. Even if you never thought about it before, if you had the chance to learn more about helping others to learn, you would probably jump at the opportunity.

d: You seem to be interested in the kind of work done by a community that lasts. Either because of things that you do or because of your personality or a little bit of both, you find yourself thinking a lot about helping to make learning and improvements in your school important and long lasting. You believe that it is important to find time for learners to test and apply what they are learning. Understanding how hard everyone is already working and how much they have to do, you try to find ways of including others without overwhelming them.

You love to learn yourself, but most of what you find yourself interested in learning about has to do with figuring out how to help your school to be a better place for teachers and students and how to help others find the time to enjoy learning as much as you do.

Rubric for Assessing the Community That Learns

A *Community That Learns* exists to help its members better understand their experiences, deepen what they know, and learn more about what they don't know.

	Beginning Community	Developing Community	Established Community	Systemic Community
Reason for and Focus of Learning Why and how the community's learning is structured	Purpose of learning is to solve a specific problem or accomplish a particular task	Purpose of learning is to improve the practice and performance of its members	Purpose of learning is to improve the learning and work of all members of the community	Purpose of learning is to improve the learning and work of all adults and students
	Content and focus of learning are predetermined for the community	Content and focus of learning are predetermined by the community	Content and focus of learning are established over time through shared conversations about individual interests and organizational needs	Content and focus of the learning are responsive to the changing expertise, interests, passions, and needs of the community and organization
	Learning is structured around new information or unfamiliar topics	Learning is structured around new information about topics of individual or group interest	Learning is related to areas of individual interest or passion	Facilitates learning that develops or deepens areas of individual expertise
Participants Who is included in the learning of the community	Learning supports individuals	Learning supports like-role groups	Supports learning in groups containing more than one role	Learning is designed for cross-role groups
Opportunities Provided for Learning When and how learning is accomplished	Learning opportunities and follow-up activities are provided at specific times and in a prescribed manner	Learning opportunities are provided at specific times, though the timing of follow-up activities may be determined at least in part by the membership of the community	Learning opportunities are provided as needed, determined by the community, with the bulk of member learning occurring independent of set meetings	Learning opportunities arise from other learning sparked by member inquiry, while scheduled time is used primarily for formal sharing of work, feedback, and discourse
	Learning opportunities are secured through outside agencies or providers	Learning opportunities may be facilitated by outside providers or other members of the organization, and not participants in the learning community itself	Learning opportunities are facilitated by members of the community who are ready to share what they are learning, or by others invited by the community	Learning opportunities are facilitated by members of the community as a way of sharing their deepening expertise and giving back to the community
	Activities ensure that everyone's learning is related to a specific, preidentified organizational need or desired outcome	Activities help individuals explore their own needs or those of their role group	Activities and processes help members connect their passions and interests with organizational needs	Activities and processes link individual visions and organizational needs and are responsive to changes in either or both

Criteria	Level 1	Level 2	Level 3	Level 4
Alignment of Community and Organization — How the community is a part of the organization	The community is seen as existing to address a specific problem or task. Outsiders view the community as a select group convened for a specific purpose	The community is seen as existing to improve practice or performance of its members. Outsiders view the community as an elite group or fraternity convened for purposes unknown	The community sees itself as existing to improve learning for all community members. Outsiders view the community as a group whose focus is to use its learning to improve practices for the betterment of the organization	The community sees itself as learning in order to improve learning for all adults and students. The community is recognized by outsiders as an entity whose learning leads to innovations and provides a model for other organizations striving to improve teaching and learning
Dispositions of Practice — How the dispositions of practice of professional learning communities are evident in the processes and work of the community	The dispositions of practice provide an intellectual challenge in comprehension. The dispositions of practice are external to and separate from the routines and practices of the community. Dispositions evidence themselves by chance in the learning and work of the community	The dispositions of practice are used as a framework for assessing themselves, their colleagues, and their work. The dispositions of practice are articulated and included in specific community activities. Dispositions are highlighted and illustrated by retrofitting them to preexisting examples of learning and work	The dispositions of practice are a compass to guide individuals' learning and work, as well as that of the community. The dispositions of practice are purposefully developed in the community through ongoing self and peer assessment, reflection, and goal setting. Dispositions are explicitly identified in ongoing learning and work	The dispositions of practice are woven into the fabric of the community, evidencing themselves in thinking, beliefs, behaviors, and work and helping the community make decisions about its learning. The dispositions of practice are embedded in all community learning and work. Dispositions are internalized and shared throughout the community
Permanence — The likelihood that the community will last beyond current initiatives or membership	The end date of the community is predetermined	The community's existence is certain only in the present, dependent on factors outside its control to determine its future	Responsibility and control over the future of the community are shared by both its membership and outside factors, but its existence can be compromised if both are not in harmony	The community has established mechanisms for responding to internal and external changes in ways that allow the community itself to maintain its viability

Rubric for Assessing the Community That Leads

A Community That Leads exists to help its members develop and deepen facilitation and leadership skills in order to support leaders who better understand how to share what they know.

	Beginning Community	Developing Community	Established Community	Systemic Community
Reason for and Focus of Learning to Lead Why and how the community's focus on leading is structured	Focus on leading is to prepare selected individuals for specific leadership roles or events Learning is geared to certifying leaders	Focus on leading is to develop an understanding of and improve leadership skills Learning is geared to developing leaders	Focus on leading is to promote best practices in leadership Learning opportunities focus on developing leadership	Focus on leading is to support leadership that will promote learning for everyone Learning opportunities focus on deepening understanding and abilities related to best practices in leadership
Participants Who is included in learning about leading	Select individuals identified as ready for formal leadership positions available in the organization	An invited cadre intended as a potential pool of leaders	Members of the community interested in formally sharing, facilitating, or leading the learning of others	All members of the learning community
Opportunities Provided for Learning When and how learning to lead is accomplished	Opportunities to lead present themselves inside the formal leadership structure of the organization Learning is secured through outside agencies or providers	Opportunities to assume leadership roles are defined and available at a variety of levels of the organization Learning may be facilitated by outside providers or by other, established leaders in the organization	Opportunities to lead emerge, sometimes at the suggestion of interested individuals, sometimes determined by a need that arises in the organization Learning may be facilitated by members of the community who are ready to share their learning about leadership or by outsiders invited by the community	Leadership opportunities evolve as the needs of the organization change and the internal expertise of its members develops Learning is facilitated by members of the community as a way of sharing their own leadership expertise and supporting the community

Alignment of Community and Organization How the community is a part of the organization	The community is viewed as an organization-sponsored academy	The community is seen as an organizational club or political entity	The community is perceived by those outside as a legitimate part of the organization	The community is recognized as the innovative core of the organization
	The community is believed to exist to fill open leadership positions in the organization	The community is viewed by those outside as an elite group being groomed to lead	The community is credited with promoting leadership practices that improve the organization as a whole	The community is a model for other organizations striving to implement leadership practices that support advances in teaching and learning
Dispositions of Practice The degree to which the dispositions of practice of professional learning communities are evident in the processes and work of the community	The dispositions of practice provide an intellectual challenge in comprehension	The dispositions of practice are used as a framework for assessing themselves, their colleagues, and their work	The dispositions of practice are a compass to guide individuals' learning and work, as well as that of the community itself	The dispositions of practice are woven into thinking, beliefs, behaviors, and work and help the community make decisions about its learning
	The dispositions of practice are external to and separate from the routines and practices of the community	The dispositions of practice are articulated and included in specific community activities	The dispositions of practice are purposefully developed in the community through ongoing self and peer assessment, reflection, and goal setting	The dispositions of practice are embedded in all community learning and work
	Dispositions evidence themselves by chance in the learning and work of the community	Dispositions are highlighted and illustrated by retrofitting them to preexisting examples of learning and work	Dispositions are explicitly identified in ongoing learning and work	Dispositions are internalized and shared throughout the community
Permanence The likelihood that the community will last beyond current initiatives or membership	The end date of the expanded community is predetermined	Membership in the community begins and ends with the current organizational need for new leaders	The future of the community is dependent on a shared appreciation for the value of cross-role learning communities in strengthening and deepening organizational leadership	The community has established mechanisms for responding to internal and external changes in ways that allow the community itself to remain viable

Rubric for Assessing the Community That Lasts

A *Community That Lasts* exists to help its members promote the resilience of their school or system to sustain positive changes and to operate as a learning organization.

	Beginning Community	Developing Community	Established Community	Systemic Community
Reason for and Focus of Learning Why and how the community's learning is structured	Purpose of learning is specific to the needs of organizing a group	Purpose of learning combines individual interest or passion with learning about how to maintain the community	Purpose of learning is connected to organizational development and funding	Purpose of learning is to develop and deepen areas of individual expertise as well as focus on questions and issues of sustainable change
	Learning focuses on what it means to learn in a community and on the relationship between and among individuals in the community	Learning focuses on the relationship between individuals and the organization	Learning and discourse are focused on questions of viability and sustainability	Learning processes and structures focus on promoting a community's sustainability and learning
Participants Who is included in the learning of the community	Individuals	Like-role groups	Groups containing more than one role	Groups representing different roles in the organization
Opportunities Provided for Learning When and how learning about lasting is accomplished	Learning opportunities and follow-up activities are provided at specific times and in a prescribed manner	Learning opportunities are provided at specific times, though the timing of follow-up activities may be determined at least in part by the membership of the community	Learning opportunities are provided on an as-needed basis, determined by the community, with the bulk of member learning occurring independent of set meetings	Learning opportunities arise from other learning sparked by member inquiry, while scheduled time is used primarily for formal sharing
	Learning opportunities are secured through outside agencies or providers	Learning opportunities may be facilitated by outside providers or other members of the organization who are not participants in the learning community itself	Learning opportunities are facilitated by members of the community who are ready to share what they are learning, or by others invited by the community	Learning opportunities are facilitated by members of the community as a way of using their expertise to address the needs of the community
	Activities support learning specific to the needs of organizing a group: scheduling meetings, securing space, and arranging for the facilitation of sessions	Activities help individuals develop basic planning skills, including planning the agenda focus and content of formal meetings	Activities and processes help members focus on funding and articulating the relationship between the vision, goals, and work of the professional learning community and the needs or problems of the organization	Activities and processes help members use strategic planning, goal setting, and monitoring processes to ensure that this and any other nested community will improve student and adult learning

Criterion				
Alignment of Community and Organization How the community that lasts is a part of the organization	The community sees itself as being responsible for chairing and regulating its members	The community sees its role mostly related to negotiating and managing members' needs and interests	The community sees its role as maintaining explicit connections between the communities that learn and lead and the organization	The community sees itself as responsible for ensuring the stability and viability of the larger community, its learning and work
	The community is seen by those outside as individuals preselected to be in charge of the group	The community is viewed by those outside as an elite group entrusted with the management of another elite group	The community is perceived by those outside as an organization whose focus is to grow and strengthen itself and its practices in order to improve the organization as a whole	The community is recognized as an entity whose focus on lasting results in innovative approaches to the sustainability of the community and its focus on improving adult and student learning
Dispositions of Practice How the dispositions of practice of professional learning communities are evident in the processes and work of the community	The dispositions of practice provide an intellectual challenge in comprehension	The dispositions of practice are used as a framework for assessing themselves, their colleagues, and their work	The dispositions of practice are a compass to guide individuals' learning, and work, as well as that of the community itself	The dispositions of practice are woven into the fabric of the community, evidencing themselves in thinking, beliefs, behaviors, and work, and helping the community make decisions about its learning
	The dispositions of practice are external to and separate from the routines and practices of the community	The dispositions of practice are articulated and included in specific community activities	The dispositions of practice are purposefully developed in the community through ongoing self and peer assessment, reflection, and goal setting	The dispositions of practice are embedded in all community learning and work
	Dispositions evidence themselves by chance in the learning and work of the community	Dispositions are highlighted and illustrated by retrofitting them to preexisting examples of learning and work	Dispositions are explicitly identified in ongoing learning and work	Dispositions are internalized and shared throughout the community
Permanence The likelihood that the community will last beyond current initiatives or membership	The end date of the community is predetermined	The community's existence is certain only in the present, dependent on factors outside its control to determine its future	Responsibility and control over the future of the community are shared by both its membership and outside factors, but its existence can be compromised if both are not in harmony	The community has established mechanisms for responding to internal and external changes in ways that allow the community itself to maintain its viability

Rubric for Assessing Student Capacity for Professional Learning Communities

Commitment to Understanding: Asking questions and developing ideas related to teaching and learning, exploring multiple perspectives, and using research and evidence

	Beginning — Commitment to Understanding May Be Present But Is Unrecognized	Developing — Commitment to Understanding Appears Inconsistently	Deepening — Commitment to Understanding is Recognized and Becoming Important	Embodying — Commitment to Understanding Is Integrated Throughout
Discourse Asking questions and developing ideas related to teaching and learning	I try to listen so I can ask the same questions as the smart kids	Other people ask better questions than I do, so I like to use their questions to help me with research	I ask different kinds of questions when I want to know different things	I try to ask questions never before asked, so I can discover something new, or find a new question
	I have lots of questions about everything	I try to find the answers to my questions, but sometimes the answer doesn't help me to know anything new	I am able to ask questions that help me learn more about something or that lead to finding new questions	I like to ask hard questions so that others and I rethink things we believe or know
Behavior and Practice Exploring multiple perspectives	Other people can think whatever they want—it doesn't change my mind about what I think or do	I like to talk to people about what I am thinking or planning to do so that they can tell me if it's a good idea	It's helpful for me to read about or talk to people with different ideas and opinions so that I can see things in different ways	It's important for me to hear or read many different points of view so I can think of interesting, original ideas or questions
	Why listen to other's ideas when I already know what I think?	If I listen to what others believe, I find that my own thinking changes to match theirs	I know what I believe, but I also think someone else may know something that's worth hearing	I believe we can learn from each other, even when we have different points of view or ideas
Work Using research and evidence	My work is based on my own ideas and experiences	I use outside information in my work	I use facts, ideas, and others' research in my work	I combine research, others' ideas, and my own thinking and experiences in my work
	I know how smart I am in a subject because of the grades that I get	I can look at my work and tell what I still need to work on	I use my work as well as the feedback that I get from my teacher and peers in order to know what needs work and to figure out a plan for improving	I use my work and my teachers' lessons and assignments to figure out what I need to do; then I use my next piece of work to see if what I tried is working

Intellectual Perseverance: Considering ideas or questions for a period of time to improve our work; revising and revising our work and our thinking to improve it and to reach high standards; and not finishing our work until it's the very best that it can be

	Beginning Intellectual Perseverance May Be Present But Is Unrecognized	*Developing* Intellectual Perseverance Appears Inconsistently	*Deepening* Intellectual Perseverance Is Recognized and Becoming Important	*Embodying* Intellectual Perseverance Is Integrated Throughout
Discourse Considering ideas or questions for a period of time to improve our work	I can see how talking about work or thinking might be helpful to some of my classmates, but I'm not really interested in that kind of thing	Sometimes I see that I need to revise my thinking or a draft of my work	I talk to my classmates about ideas I have for rethinking or revising my work	I ask my classmates and teacher for their ideas about what I might do to improve my thinking or work
	There is so much to think and talk about that it's hard to concentrate on any one idea or question for very long	I'm okay discussing ideas that others want to talk about, but I don't usually think much about them afterward unless somebody brings them up again	I'll discuss my own and others' ideas or questions anytime, especially when they have to do with things I need or care about	I enjoy starting and continuing debates and conversations with my friends, especially about questions that challenge what some believe and do
Behavior and Practice Revising our work and our thinking to improve it and to reach high standards	I try to do what I know I'm supposed to do in school, but what I really like most is getting to spend time with my friends	I like to see my work used as a model or used in meetings or to decorate the school	I think that I can help my school by participating in clubs and school government	I believe that I can make a difference in my school, and I will work as hard as I can to do so
	I believe that my first ideas are good enough, so I don't see the need to revise my work	If revising my work is what I have to do for it to be considered done, then I will do it	I like to revise and improve my work to make it closer to what the teacher wants and so I can get a better grade	I will change and improve my work until it's as close to perfect as I can make it
Work Not saying that work is finished until it's the very best that it can be	The work that I hand in is virtually the same as my original draft	I am able to see what I need to revise in my own work	I revise my thinking and my work in order to correct the problems I know about	I rethink or revise my work so much that I end up with lots of drafts, and each one is a little bit better than the one before it
	I find other things to do when we are given time to revise	I am willing to revise my work during class	I try to find the time to revise my work, even if it means making time outside class	I will make as many revisions as it takes for my work to be the best that it can be, even if it's almost time to hand it in and I have to stay up all night

Courage and Initiative: Discussing uncomfortable topics or issues, including own values and questions; being okay with the difficulties and discomfort of changing; accepting new or unfamiliar roles, responsibilities, or challenges

	Beginning Courage and Initiative May Be Present But Are Unrecognized	*Developing* Courage and Initiative Appear Inconsistently	*Deepening* Courage and Initiative Are Recognized and Becoming Important	*Embodying* Courage and Initiative Are Integrated Throughout
Discourse Discussing uncomfortable topics or issues, including own values and questions	I'll share my ideas, assumptions, and beliefs if asked, but I have no idea what to do about them	I'll share my values, beliefs, and assumptions when I know that's what I'm supposed to do	I'm fine with sharing what I believe, value, and assume and with what I think can be done	I especially like to play devil's advocate, using my values, beliefs, and ideas to spark conversation
	I hesitate to ask for explanations and ask questions only when I'm told I have to	I'll ask questions but only when others have done so first	I don't think twice about asking questions that show what I do not know	I'm at ease asking questions that show what I don't know and try to help others do the same
	I identify issues or questions that require no discussion	I agree or disagree in discussions on issues or questions	I raise questions in conversations and discussions	I state beliefs and questions, even when they may make others uncomfortable
Behavior and Practice Being okay with the difficulties and discomfort of changing	I avoid people or activities that make me uncomfortable about what I know or believe	I won't participate in activities that raise difficult questions for me, but I will listen or watch others do that	I don't avoid things that make me uncomfortable or question my beliefs or actions; I focus on dealing with them	I look forward to having my thinking or beliefs challenged enough to make me uncomfortable
	I prefer not to share my work because it's not good enough, and I don't want to waste anyone's time	I spend lots of time polishing my work when I know we'll be sharing, and then I try to share last	I share my work whenever I have the chance, whether it's complete or unfinished	I share my work at any stage if I think it might help me to figure out what to work on next
	I go to my teacher, another adult, or an older student for answers or help with problems so I know what to do	I ask for help any time there is an issue or a problem that causes an argument	I try to help people solve their problems and stop disagreeing or arguing so that everyone get along	I try to help people talk things out, even if it makes them uncomfortable or if it will start an argument
Work Seeking or accepting new or unfamiliar roles	I don't like change; I want things and people to stay just as they are right now, no matter what	I am willing to take on new jobs in my class or school, but it makes me a little bit nervous	I look for new jobs or roles in my class and school, because I think I can learn a lot from doing something different	I look for ways to challenge myself by doing things I have never done before and taking on new roles and responsibilities
	My work and ideas fit what I know people expect	My work and ideas define what is accepted or expected	My work and ideas raise questions of what is accepted or expected	My work and ideas challenge what is accepted or expected

Commitment to Reflection: Sharing our thinking to develop and evaluate it; thinking about our thinking and learning to set goals, assess, and understand ourselves, our work, and our school; producing work that results from goals, actions, and strategies that are based on the analysis of past learning

	Beginning Commitment to Reflection May Be Present But Is Unrecognized	*Developing* Commitment to Reflection Appears Inconsistently in Discourse, Behavior, and work	*Deepening* Commitment to Reflection Is Present, Recognized, and Becoming Important	*Embodying* Commitment to Reflection Is Integrated into Discourse, Behavior, and Work
Discourse Sharing our thinking to develop and evaluate it	I need questions or some ideas to help me communicate my thinking about myself and my work I'm careful about how and with whom I share questions related to my work and thinking I have too many ideas about things I want to change and do to be able to talk about them with others	When we're assigned time to self-assess, I can evaluate my work and discuss what I see on my own I have no trouble talking about the questions I have about my work and thinking When we talk about goals, other people's seem more important or interesting, so I want to change mine	If someone asks, I can explain what my work is about, what it still needs, and how good it is I share my questions with others and connect them to specific actions that will improve my work and thinking Discussing my goals helps me to connect them more closely to my learning and work	I find myself constantly asking questions about whether what I am thinking or doing is good enough and where it can be better I can discuss what I am thinking and questioning and give specific examples of how it's affecting my work Conversations with others about goals and plans to achieve them help us all to become clearer and to see where they might be related
Behavior and Practice Thinking about our thinking and learning to set goals, assess, and understand ourselves, our work, and our school	I realize that there are things that I should be doing better When I think about the things that I can do to my work, I always consider how difficult they might be	I can identify general strengths and weaknesses in my own work I try to think about how what I do will improve my work	I am able to assess the specific strengths and weaknesses of my own work I think about how what I do might help me get closer to my goals	I can assess and discuss my thinking and work and use that to set future goals I think carefully about what I'm going to do and try to imagine everything that could possibly happen as a result
Work Producing work that results from goals, actions, and strategies that are based on the analysis of past learning	I'm sure I could find some patterns in other people's work, but I don't see why that's important to me	I recognize patterns and relationships when someone points them out to me	I look for patterns and relationships in my own thinking and work	When I assess my work, I look carefully for patterns and relationships, and use them to help me make improvements

Commitment to Expertise: Refining and expanding our current knowledge and skills; disseminating our knowledge and expertise within and outside our own school; engaging in work that addresses school or learning needs

	Beginning Commitment to Expertise May Be Present But Is Unrecognized	*Developing* Commitment to Expertise Appears Inconsistently in Discourse, Behavior, and Work	*Deepening* Commitment to Expertise Is Present, Recognized, and Becoming Important	*Embodying* Commitment to Expertise Is Integrated into Discourse, Behavior, and Work
Discourse Refining and expanding our current knowledge and skills	I will do research if I am assigned a question or focus I like doing things that I already know and understand	I prefer to do research myself, so I can focus on what interests me I like to learn new things	I prefer to be involved in activities that make me answer questions in order to understand more I like to get really good at doing one thing before I try to do something else, and I will work hard to accomplish that	I like individual and group research as well as activities to improve my understanding, especially when what I learn or do could help others I love to learn new things that help me ask better questions about what I already know or help me to think and do things differently
Behavior and Practice Disseminating our knowledge and expertise within and outside our own organization	I know that I have to learn and improve I do what I am told to do, when I'm supposed to do it	I realize that I have a lot to learn, and I think that's what school is for I can work and learn by myself, in study or cooperative groups, if someone tells me to	I am learning a lot, but I'm not sure that I know enough about anything yet to be able to teach it to someone else I look forward to the chance to learn in different ways, individually or with others	I have learned a lot, and though I realize I still have a lot more to learn, I think other people might be helped by what I already know I find ways to get different opportunities for myself and others to question, work, and learn things that we're interested in
Work Disseminating our knowledge and expertise within and outside our own school	I dread the idea of presenting my work I don't feel comfortable or ready to share what I am learning	Presenting or sharing my work is something I know I have to do I can share what I have learned with my peers	Presenting my work is an important responsibility I can share what I have learned with my peers and with other students whom I may not know well	Presenting my work is something I should do as part of being a learner I am willing to share what I learn with others, even if they are from outside my school

Collegiality: Learning with and from others; believing that learning and working with others makes us smarter; producing work that results from engaging in collaborative learning and problem solving

	Beginning — Collegiality May Be Present But Is Unrecognized	Developing — Collegiality Appears Inconsistently in Discourse, Behavior, and Work	Deepening — Collegiality Is Present, Recognized, and Becoming Important	Embodying — Collegiality Is Integrated into Discourse, Behavior, and Work
Discourse Learning with and from others	I know that people will talk to me about my questions and learning, but I prefer to think alone	I am curious about what other students are doing or trying	I am interested in learning from other students who know more than I do about something	I want to learn, but I also want to feel that I am adding to what others know or can do
Behavior and Practice Acting on the belief that learning and working with others increases our expertise	I can think and talk about what works best for me as a learner when I have to	When someone asks or seems interested, I think and talk about what works best for me as a learner	I like having opportunities to explore and discuss what works best for me as a learner	I help myself and others to understand, develop, and explain what works best for us as learners
	I will give and take help when it seems needed	I easily offer and ask for help during times like conferences or peer feedback sessions	I look for opportunities to offer and ask for help when I need it	I ask for the chance to be involved in shared learning and in helping others with their work
Work Engaging in collaborative learning and problem solving to produce work	I will share my work when asked to	I will share my work with others in order to learn something that will help me to do better	I'll share my work with others, and I try to get them to do the same, even if what we're sharing isn't something we each need at the time	I share my work and thinking in order to support others' learning, as well as my own
	I prefer to work alone, without help or interference from other people	I don't mind working with others, but it's hard for me to figure out how to combine their ideas with mine	I enjoy working with others and hearing what they have to say	I look for others to share ideas with so that I can hear lots of different points of view about my work or thinking

Bandura, A. "Perceived Self-Efficacy in Cognitive Development and Functioning." *Educational Psychologist,* 1993, *28*(2), 117–148.

Blythe, T., Allen, D., and Powell, B. S. *Looking Together at Students' Work: A Companion Guide to Assessing Student Learning.* New York: Teachers College Press, 1999.

Brandt, R. "Professional Learning Communities: An Overview." In S. Hord (ed.), *Learning Together: Leading Together: Changing Schools Through Professional Learning Communities.* New York: Teachers College Press, 2004.

Byme, C. J. "Teacher Knowledge and Teacher Effectiveness: A Literature Review Theoretical Analysis and Discussion of Research Strategy." Paper presented at the meeting of the Northern Educational Research Association, Ellenville, N.Y., 1983.

Capers, M. "A History of Resistance; A Future Dependent on Its Embrace." In S. Hord (ed.), *Learning Together: Leading Together: Changing Schools Through Professional Learning Communities.* New York: Teachers College Press, 2004.

Carnegie Forum on Education and the Economy. *A Nation Prepared: Teachers for the Twenty-First Century.* New York: Carnegie Corporation of New York, 1986.

Darling-Hammond, L. "Enhancing Teaching." In W. Owings and L. Kaplan (eds.), *Best Practices, Best Thinking, and Emerging Issues in School Leadership.* Thousand Oaks, Calif.: Corwin Press, 2003.

Dreyfus, H., and Dreyfus, S. *Mind over Machine: The Power of Human Intuition and Expertise in the Era of the Computer.* New York: Free Press, 1986.

DuFour, R., DuFour, R., Eaker, R., and Many, T. *Learning by Doing: A Handbook of Professional Learning Communities at Work.* Bloomington, Ind.: Solution Tree, 2006.

DuFour, R., Eaker, R., and DuFour, R. *On Common Ground: The Power of Professional Learning Communities.* Bloomington, Ind.: National Educational Service, 2005.

Fieman-Nemser, S., and Floden, R. E. "The Cultures of Teaching." In M. Wittrock (ed.), *Handbook of Research on Teaching* (pp. 505–526). New York: Macmillan, 1986.

Fletcher, A. *Meaningful Student Involvement: A Guide to Students as Partners in School Change.* Olympia, Wash.: Freechild Project, 2005.

Fullan, M. "Professional Learning Communities Writ Large." In R. DuFour, R. Eaker, and R. DuFour (eds.), *On Common Ground: The Power of Professional Learning Communities.* Bloomington, Ind.: National Educational Service, 2005.

Goddard, R. D., Hoy, W. K., and Hoy, A. W. "Collective Teacher Efficacy: Its Meaning, Measure, and Impact on Student Achievement." *American Educational Research Journal,* 2000, *27*(2), 479–507.

Hargreaves, A., and Macmillan, R. "Balkanized Secondary Schools and the Malaise of Modernity." Paper presented at the Annual Meeting of the American Educational Research Association, San Francisco, Apr. 1991.

Hargreaves, D. "Working Laterally: How Innovation Networks Make an Education Epidemic." *Demos Innovation.* Retrieved Oct. 15, 2005, from http://www.standards. dfes.gov.uk/innovation-unit. 2003.

Hord, S. (ed.). *Learning Together: Leading Together: Changing Schools Through Professional Learning Communities.* New York: Teachers College Press, 2004.

King, B. M., and Newmann, F. M. "Building School Capacity Through Professional Development: Conceptual and Empirical Considerations." *International Journal of Educational Management,* 2001, *15*(2), 86–93.

Lambert, L. "Leadership for Lasting Reform." *Educational Leadership,* Feb. 2005, pp. 62–65.

Lieberman, A., and Miller, L. *Teacher Leadership.* San Francisco: Jossey-Bass, 2004.

Little, J. W. "District Policy Choices and Teachers' Professional Development Opportunities." *Educational Evaluation and Policy Analysis,* 1989, *11*(2), 165–179.

Little, J. W. "Inside Teacher Community: Representations of Classroom Practice." *Teachers College Record,* 2003, *105,* 913–945.

Louis, K., and Kruse, S. "Professional Learning Communities: An Overview." In S. Hord (ed.), *Learning Together: Leading Together: Changing Schools Through Professional Learning Communities.* New York: Teachers College Press, 1995.

McDonald, J., Mohr, N., Dichter, A., and McDonald, E. *The Power of Protocols: An Educator's Guide to Better Practice.* New York: Teachers College Press, 2003.

McLaughlin, M. W., and Talbert, J. E. *Professional Communities and the Work of High School Teaching.* Chicago: University of Chicago Press, 2001.

Moller, G., and others. "Teacher Leadership: A Product of Supportive and Shared Leadership Within Professional Learning Communities." Paper presented at the Annual Meeting of the American Educational Research Association, New Orleans, Apr. 2000.

Munro, J. *Professional Learning Teams: Building the Capacity for Improving Teaching and Learning.* Melbourne, Australia: National College for School Leadership, 2005.

National Board for Professional Teacher Standards. "What Teachers Should Know and Be Able to Do: The Five Core Propositions." Retrieved from http://www.nbpts.org/ about/coreprops. 2001

National Commission on Teaching and America's Future. *What Matters Most: Teaching for America's Future.* New York: National Commission on Teaching and America's Future, 1996.

O'Day, J. "Complexity, Accountability and School Improvement." In S. H. Fuhrman and R. F. Elmore (eds.), *Redesigning Accountability Systems for Education.* New York: Teachers College Press, 2004.

Ritchhart, R. "From IQ to IC: A Dispositional View of Intelligence." *Roeper Review,* 2001, *23*(3), 143–150.

Ross, J. A., and Gray, P. "Transformation Leadership and Teacher Commitment to Organizational Values: The Mediating Effects of Collective Teacher Efficacy." *School Effectiveness and School Improvement,* 2006, *17*(2), 179–199.

Senge, P. *The Fifth Discipline.* New York: Doubleday, 1990.

Sergiovanni, T. J. *"Leadership as Cultural Expression."* In T. J. Sergiovanni and J. E. Corballi (eds.), *Leadership and Organizational Culture* (pp. 105–144). Urbana: University of Illinois Press, 1994.

Shulman, L. S. *The Wisdom of Practice: Essays on Teaching, Learning and Learning to Teach.* San Francisco: Jossey-Bass, 2004.

Shulman, L. S., and Carey, N. "Psychology and Limitations of Individual Rationality: Implications for the Study of Reasoning and Civility," *Review of Educational Research,* 1984, *54,* 501–524.

Silins, H., and Mulford, B. "Schools as Learning Organizations—Effects of Teacher Leadership and Student Outcomes." *School Effectiveness and School Improvement,* 2004, *15*(3), 443–466.

Sparks, D. "Leading for Transformation in Teaching, Learning and Relationships." In R. DuFour, R. Eaker, and R. DuFour (eds.), *On Common Ground: The Power of Professional Learning Communities.* Bloomington, Ind.: National Educational Service, 2005.

Spillane, J. *Distributed Leadership.* San Francisco: Jossey-Bass, 2006.

Strong, R. Presentation at the Center for the Study of Expertise in Teaching and Learning, Long Island, N.Y., Mar., 2007.

Vygotsky, L. S. *Thought and Language.* Cambridge, Mass.: MIT Press, 1962.

Wenger, E. *Communities of Practice: Learning, Meaning and Identity.* Cambridge: Cambridge University Press, 1998.

Wenger, E. "Communities of Practice. Learning as a Social System." *Systems Thinker.* Retrieved from http://www.co-i-l.com/coil/knowledge-garden/cop/lss.shtml. 1998.

Yankelovich, D. *The Magic of Dialogue: Transforming Conflict into Cooperation.* New York: Touchstone, 2001.

York-Barr, J., and Duke, K. "What Do We Know About Teacher Leadership? Findings from Two Decades of Scholarship." *Review of Educational Research,* 2004, *74*(3), 255–316.

attempts at, learning from, 153

Educational resources, issue of, 3

Efficiency, valuing, issue of, 28

Embodying level: of Collegiality, *161*, *197*; of Commitment to Expertise, *46*, *160*, *196*; of Commitment to Reflection, *141*, *159*, *195*; of Commitment to Understanding, *37*, *38*, *156*, *192*; of Courage and Initiative, *42*, *158*, *194*; of dispositions of practice, 35; of Intellectual Perseverance, *40*, *157*, *193*

Established level: in communities that last, *97*, *188–189*; in communities that lead, *97*, *184–185*; in communities that learn, *180–181*; of involvement, *136*; in professional learning communities, 27, 82–83, 85, 108, *136*

Evidence: identifying, 144; self-assessment accompanied by, 140, *141*, 142, 143, 149. *See also* Artifacts

Exemplars: role of, 130–131; use of, 119

Expertise: articulation of, 91; assertion of, issue with, 46–47, 49; capitalizing on, failure at, 15; cultivating individual and collective, 82; developing, critical role in, 104; harnessing, 13; increasing, importance of, 10; list defining educator, *50*; potential for, harnessing, 153; reflection by an educator on, *51*; table of, 47, *48*. *See also* Commitment to Expertise

Expertise and growth, evaluating. *See* Participant evaluation

"Expertise Equalizer," *51*

F

Facilitation: of alignment, 83–85; context for, 78–81; of learning opportunities, 82–83; of participation and membership, 81–82; of start-up and operation processes, 86–96

Facilitators: negotiation by, of roles relative to positional leadership, 82; participants as, 92; roles and responsibilities of, 86–87, 105

Fads, 4

Feedback: on a draft agenda, 93, *94*; protocol for, example of, *106–107*; on rationale, example of, 127, *128*; role of, 104–105, 107, 129

Feedback and Refinement Stage, 142

Feige, D. M., 47, *48*, 144–145

Fields, R., 19

Fieman-Nemser, S., 14

Fletcher, A., 118

Flexible and responsive program design, assessing, 123, *124*

Floden, R. E., 14

Focus: defining purpose and, 78–81; self-assessment of, 171–172

Formal application and induction process, use of, 135, 138–139

Formative device, 135

Fullan, M., 17

Fuller, A., 44

Future practice, *8*

G

Gamberg, M. E., 36

Glickman, S., 47, *48*

Goals and action plans, revising, 107–108

Goddard, R. D., 10, 15

Gray, P., 4, 14

Gray, T., 145

Growth: of communities, assessment of, 98, *99–100*; reflection on, *7–8*

151–154; scenarios depicting, 1–2, 6–7, 19–20, 20–21, 111–112; schools benefiting from, 13–16; students benefiting from, 9–11; teachers benefiting from, 11–13, 16; underlying tenet of, 9. *See also specific aspects of professional learning communities*

Purpose: assessment focused on, 96, *97*; and focus, defining, 78–81; as a key variable, 19–25; shared, 82, 109

Q

Questions, generating, to provide evidence of dispositions, 140, 142–143

R

Rating scales, use of, 98, *99–100*

Rationale: curriculum, 119, 121, 122–123; feedback on, example of, 127, *128*; for professional learning communities, 2–3; revised, example of, 127–128

Readiness, concept of, 33

Readiness factors, 34

Readiness, individual and organizational, development of. *See*

Individual capacity; Organizational capacity

Readiness, lack of. *See* Prereadiness

Readiness-capacity continuum, various levels on the. *See* Beginning level; Deepening level; Developing level; Embodying level; Established level; Systemic level

Recruiting and inducting members: issues in, 87–88; measures useful for, 134–135, *136*; role of facilitator in, 86; tool for, 88, 171–177

"Reflective Toolbox," 140

Reflection prompts, example of, *146*

Reflective practice, 6, 27, *48*, 143. *See also* Commitment to Reflection

Reflective practitioner, participant as, 90–91

Reform: educational, 4, 153; school, 13–14, 15, 153

Repositioning, 109

Research and development work, devotion to, importance of, 152–153

Research and inquiry, in a sample table of expertise, *48*

Research work, revision process needed for a shift in, annotated exemplar of the, 130–131

Researcher, participant as, 91

Responsibility, collective, 58

Résumés, submitting, 139

Rich text protocol for a discussion, 93, *95–96*

Ritchhart, R., 29

Roles and responsibilities: assigning, 56; of facilitators, 86–87, 105; leadership, helping participants identify, 84

Ross, J. A., 4, 14

Rubrics: certification, example of, related to Intellectual Persever-ance, *147–148*, 149; for communities that last, 96, *97*, 187–189; for communities that lead, 96, *97*, 183–185; for communities that learn, 96, 179–181; for curriculum rationales, 119, *122*; for design of action research studies, *126*; for flexibility in program design, 123, *124*; for individual capacity, 135, 155–161; for organizational capacity, 163–169; for rationales to structure feedback, 127, *128*; for student capacity, 89,

Turnaround Leadership

Michael Fullan

Paper ISBN: 978-0-7879-6985-1
www.josseybass.com

"*Michael Fullan goes beyond a critique of contemporary practice to offer specific, comprehensive strategies to create schools that become continuously more effective by building the capacity and the confidence of the educators within them. This is a must read for anyone serious about meaningful school improvement.*"

—**Richard DuFour, educational author and consultant**

"*Michael Fullan moves with authority to identify the kind of leadership needed to turn around our schools. His turnaround solutions are not the product of armchair contemplation, but have emerged out of the sweat and tears of actual systemic reform efforts.*"

—**Peter Hill, secretary general of the Hong Kong Examinations and Assessment Authority**

"*Fullan goes far beyond the rhetoric of moral purpose to lay out in stark terms what he rightly calls the 'real reform' agenda.*"

—**David Hopkins, HSBC chair of international leadership, Institute of Education, University of London**

In *Turnaround Leadership*, Michael Fullan, an internationally recognized leader on educational reform, expands the definition of organizational turnaround and shows how leaders can convert even the worst situation into an opportunity to shake-up and rejuvenate their schools. Indeed he goes beyond turnaround schools to show how entire systems can be transformed.

Fullan examines the dynamics of what makes societies—and education systems—healthy or sick. He identifies the positive things turnaround schools do to get off the critical list, and explores what it takes to motivate large numbers of people to go beyond short-term solutions in order to achieve fundamental, sustainable reform. Ultimately, *Turnaround Leadership* focuses on the critical role of leadership—not the Lone Ranger leader who rides into town and saves a single school, but leaders whose very actions change the systems they work in.

This is a volume in the Jossey-Bass Leadership Library in Education—a series designed to meet the demand for new ideas and insights about leadership in schools.

Michael Fullan is professor of policy studies at the Ontario Institute for Studies in Education of the University of Toronto. Recognized as an international authority on educational reform, he is engaged in training, consulting, and evaluating change projects around the world. Fullan is also author of *Leading in a Culture of Change* and *The Six Secrets of Change.*

Leading in a Culture of Change

Michael Fullan

Paper   ISBN: 978-0-7879-8766-4
www.josseybass.com

"Leading in a Culture of Change *provides some sensible, practical, and sometimes provocative insights into leadership in a rapidly changing culture . . . [It] will be of great value to anyone in the field of management but also educators or educational administrators.*"
—Journal of Business and Finance Leadership

"*This is a book for all would-be heads of department and deputy heads. Every serving head should buy a copy. I shall buy at least 50 and enjoy giving them away to those at the start of their careers in the confident knowledge that the next generation will be more successful as leaders than the present one.*"
—Times Education Supplement

"*At the very time the need for effective leadership is reaching critical proportions, Michael Fullan's* Leading in a Culture of Change *provides powerful insights for moving forward. We look forward to sharing it with our grantees.*"
—Tom Vander Ark, executive director, Education, Bill and Melinda Gates Foundation

Business, nonprofit, and public sector leaders are facing new and daunting challenges—rapid-paced developments in technology, sudden shifts in the marketplace, and crisis and contention in the public arena. If they are to survive in this chaotic environment, leaders must develop the skills they need to lead effectively no matter how fast the world around them is changing.

Leading in a Culture of Change offers new and seasoned leaders' insights into the dynamics of change and presents a unique and imaginative approach for navigating the intricacies of the change process. Michael Fullan—an internationally acclaimed expert in organizational change—shows how leaders in all types of organizations can accomplish their goals and become exceptional leaders. He draws on the most current ideas and theories on the topic of effective leadership, incorporates case examples of large scale transformation, and reveals a remarkable convergence of powerful themes or, as he calls them, the five core competencies.

By integrating the five core competencies—attending to a broader moral purpose, keeping on top of the change process, cultivating relationships, sharing knowledge, and setting a vision and context for creating coherence in organizations—leaders will be empowered to deal with complex change. They will be transformed into exceptional leaders who consistently mobilize their compatriots to do important and difficult work under conditions of constant change.

Also available: *Leading in a Culture of Change Personal Action Guide and Workbook* (978-0-7879-6969-1).